Real Estate Investing

An Essential Guide to Flipping Houses, Wholesaling Properties and Building a Rental Property Empire, Including Tips for Finding Quick Profit Deals and Passive Income Assets

Contents

Introduction

Real estate is a massive industry. Totaling to a multi-trillion-dollar market, it continues to expand and become a significant part of life. Typically, real estate investment is simple. The goal is to invest money, and give it time to increase, in the future, you will have a lot of money. While each type of investment demands some level of risk, the expected profit must secure the level of risk expected. For example, consider the game of monopoly. To win, a person has to buy properties, avoid getting bankrupt, and collect rent to build more properties. If only real estate were that easy, then everyone would be rich. In life, the same concept applies, but there is a catch: a single mistake in your investment process will result in severe consequences.

There are several places that you can hide your money than under your pillow. There are positives and negative features of every investment option you take, but since this book is about real estate investment, that is what is going to focus on.

One of the most popular reasons that people say when asked why they want to invest in real estate is that they want financial freedom, but there are others as well who have their reasons why. Whatever reason you may have, if you are new to real estate investing, and want to learn how to invest in real estate, this book is perfect for you.

In this book, you will learn an overview of real estate investment, then dive deep into making money through flipping houses, wholesaling properties, and how to build a rental property empire. Also, you will learn valuable tips to use to find quick profit deals.

Chapter 1: Overview of Real Estate

To successfully build an investment opportunity the in real estate market, you need to conduct due diligence to make sure that you know the subtle details of your local market and aspects that determine the profitability of what you are investing.

This chapter will take you through a broad introduction of everything that you need to know about investing in real estate.

At a basic level, real estate investing is defined as a means of generating income by renting or owning residential, commercial, and industrial properties, or parcels of land. Some investors may look for these properties on their own, or even with the help of online real estate marketplaces such as Zillow, Multiple Listing Services, and Roofstock.

Residential real estate investments are one of the most common types of real estate investing. They comprise of single-family homes, townhomes, and condos that can be rented out to make a profit.

Larger residential properties and those meant for businesses belong to the commercial real estate category. Owners can generate money from commercial properties by leasing out multi-family units or office space.

The main point is that anything that is rented out to a business, and any residential building that has more than four units inside it, is categorized as commercial. These kinds of properties have different lending rules when registering for a mortgage.

No matter the type of property that you own, you can make some profit from an investment property in four main ways: appreciation, rent, tax benefits, and interest.

Rent

The owner of a crowdfunded real estate, townhome, condo, single-family home, multi-family property, or commercial building may create rental income by leasing out all or a section of the building to a tenant. Most people who invest in real estate decide to rent a space to tenants because it generates a predictable, steady, and consistent revenue stream.

This is especially true if you are located in a stable real estate market. Make sure to confirm the local vacancy rates on the kind of real estate property you would like to invest.

Some people decide to pocket rent and deal with property maintenance and upkeep on their own, while others choose to recruit a property management company that takes part of the profits in exchange for property management services.

Averagely, you can estimate that a property manager will require 10% of your gross rent, for long-term renters. When managing short-term rentals, this number is much bigger.

Appreciation

In some real estate markets where the cost of the property is increasing, owners of properties can make money by buying and holding the property. The rise in the value of a property over time is referred to as appreciation. Appreciation translates into profit when the owner opts to sell the property.

This strategy of earning a profit is best suited for people who are searching for a long-term investment in a market where property prices keep increasing. A long-term buy-and-hold plan is always the best choice, given that in a long-term deal, real estate prices will appreciate.

Tax Benefits

One of the most important aspects considered by real estate investors that most newbies fail to recognize is the tax benefits. Being a real estate investor is like a business owner; you receive tax deductions.

That includes any improvements to the property, the cost of travel, supplies for cleaning and maintenance, and so on.

However, the best thing of all about investing in real estate is depreciation. This is a magical feature that every investor should collect at the end of the tax year.

Depreciation implies that the IRS allows people with investment properties to "depreciate" the property over a specific period. Most importantly, the IRS should allow investors to depreciate property over 27.5 years.

Interest

This strategy of real estate profit creation is often applied by private equity firms and real estate investment firms. Someone will grant a real estate loan to a real estate developer to buy property and then gather interest and fees to generate revenue.

In the following case, you will be acting as a bank, which is perfect for a real estate investing technique.

Is Real Estate Investing Best For You?

Investing in real estate may sound like a reasonably attractive idea. After all, who doesn't want to make some extra money?

But the truth is that it is not for everyone. Some people are perfect for real estate investing, and others do well with alternative options of investment—if you are looking for a hands-off approach to real estate, you can test crowdfunded real estate options through Fundrise.

Fundrise will let individual investors invest in commercial real estate online via a Real Estate Investment Trust or an eFund. The crowdsourcing model distinguishes them from a traditional REIT, making it possible for the average investor to take part. The best thing is that you do not need to be an accredited investor. You can start to invest in deals as little as $500.

If you want to know whether this may be the right option for you, the following questions may help:

Do You Have The Right Skills For Real Estate Investing?

Unlike other investments, investing in real estate calls for accurate computations and regular monitoring of the market. You may also have to deal with the daily upkeep and property maintenance with other service providers, which can be challenging and time-consuming.

Ask yourself whether you have the organizational skills, market knowledge, and motivation to invest in real estate before you make a decision.

Are You In A Favorable Market?

Even if you have all the skills, knowledge, and capital on paper to begin investing in real estate, it does not translate to a great idea. If the market is declining or is at the top of a bull market, then you will not make a profit from a real estate investment.

However, even if your market is declining, you can still look for investment opportunities outside your area and buy properties in a more favorable place. Roofstock is an excellent platform for finding market opportunities.

Do You Have The Resources To Invest?

You should not invest money into a down payment that you are not ready to lose, so don't rush for an investment property that would lead you into financial distress.

Can You Handle The Commitment That Comes With Investment?

If you decide to rent or lease a property, get ready to handle all the tasks that come along with that. You will need to deal with rent collection, repairs, maintenance, and other related tasks.

Ask yourself whether you can handle these responsibilities. If not, you should be ready to contact a company and pay them for assistance.

Challenge

There is much uncertainty in the way investors can participate in property investing. Consumers don't know how they can take part in allocating a given portion of their portfolio to real estate without taking part in intangible assets.

With a few options to choose from, investors can sometimes be confused about which opportunity they should take.

So Why Invest In real Estate?

Real estate can be an excellent way for one to realize their financial goals. However, before you can build wealth through real estate investment, you will need to be well informed about it. As an investor, you need to ask yourself this question: "Why real estate?"

A Secure Option

There is no argument that real estate is a far much better option compared to stock market investments. For example, you can buy-and-hold property, and be sure to make a profit when you sell the same property after two, three, or even five years.

Leverage

Leverage is the best strategy to use to increase your dollar investment. If you decide to invest in real estate, you can also choose to borrow against your property. That means you will pay a down payment in the range of 20—25% for your investment.

Inflation Hedging

The trend in real estate involves losing a small value when the prices go up. However, it has a high value during times of inflation. Assets of real estate work better than paper assets, and this makes it the best inflation hedge than stocks. The reason is that real estate has an intrinsic value, whereas shares do not.

Theory Of Supply And Demand

It is clear that the rate of population growth across the world keeps increasing every year. However, land continues to be limited. As a result, house prices will continue to rise because of high demand.

Passive Income

Investing in real estate generates a positive cash flow as long as you choose the right investment. It means that real estate investment can be a great way to earn passive income.

No Restrictions Put On Investing

Anyone is free to invest in real estate. If you have the skills required to become a real estate investor, you are free to get started.

Small Capital Needed To Invest

Another reason why you should invest in real estate is that you don't need to have millions of dollars in your bank. If you can pay a down payment of between 20-25%, then you will be good to go.

Ways To Invest In Real Estate

Now that you have learned why you need to invest in real estate, we want to look at how you can get started. One thing you should know is that there are different strategies to use to invest in real estate.

Chapter 2: Flipping Houses

Flipping houses is currently the most popular technique of real estate investing. But before we proceed, what is house flipping?

Simply put, this is the process of purchasing distressed properties, renovating and repairing them, and selling the improved property to a new homeowner at a higher price than what you bought it for.

The way house flipping is done these days is far more profitable and rewarding than in the past. When you purchase ugly, gutted properties, and beautifully renovate them, and then responsibly sell them, not only will you be adding genuine value to the community, but you are also making significant profits.

However, as simple as it may sound, there are many steps that you need to follow and implement. Forgetting even a single step may lead to problems. To that point, the worst mistake you can make is to dive right in without a clue of what you are going to do. If you don't know where to start, or you need a refresher course, this chapter will teach you everything about flipping real estate.

The Basics

Let's get started by clearing up some confusion with terms, and ensure that flipping a house is the right thing for you to dive into.

Flipping is also known as:

- Fix and flip

- Buy-to-sell

- Trading

"Buy-to-sell" is perhaps the most common term because it emphasizes the intention and differentiates it from "buy-to-let". But most people prefer the term "flip" maybe because it is a simple word to say.

Well, flipping may not necessarily mean renovating a property as some people think. In fact, to some, the term "flipping" refers to situations where you are not doing any work. For example, you buy a property at a more significant discount and immediately return it to the market.

Typically, there would be a reason to explain the higher sale price, and that cannot be the growth of capital because both the purchase and sale are often months apart instead of years. For that reason, improving the property is always part of the flip process, but it's not a must for it to be. You can also increase the value by:

- Resolving legal problems

- Flat-out purchasing a bargain

- Extending a lease

So Why Flip?

If you are thinking of flipping houses for your real estate investment, there are many great questions that you will need to ask, and one of the many that you should ask is: "Why flip houses?" Let's look at some general reasons why people flip houses.

It looks like it requires a great deal of work, and it is. It is not as easy as you may think, although most people around the world buy houses every day with the ultimate reason in mind to flip those houses. Why? Making large sums of money is the long and short answer, but it is more in-depth than that for many who desire to flip houses even if making a profit is the end goal.

Some people experience pleasure and satisfaction in working with their minds. Buying a property that requires some cosmetic repairs and renovation is a great way to get your hands dirty without risking a lot of money, effort, or time. Properties that demand serious work may need a pair of hands that have some experience instead of hands that are best at balancing books. That said, if you want to do the work on your own and enjoy the idea that you can save some sizable amount of money if you use your labor, then you should go for it.

However, some people dive into flipping houses because the prospect of building their family a dream house is nice. When you purchase a home and flip it, you are putting your sweat into fulfilling someone else's dream. You are taking something that may have been looking ugly and plain and converting it into a beautiful home. While this may appear a bit romantic, it is a reason. And this is part of the beauty of flipping houses.

Others choose this line because they want to experience the pain that goes into converting a lump of coal into a diamond. The literal term for this kind of people, and this could also apply for anyone who chooses to flip houses for a living, is a masochist.

There are those who are only motivated by profit—and there is nothing wrong with that. Most people will never have gotten into this type of business if there was no pot of gold awarded on the other side of the rainbow. It is backbreaking work, and there are times when the motivation of a profit will wake you out of bed and make you hit the ground running yet again.

Keep in mind that when the sun sets, it does not matter what your reason for flipping houses is. The most important thing is that you do the work necessary to pull off your house flip day after day. This is what distinguishes those who are serious at flipping houses and those who are doomed to be one-hit wonders in this business. Of course, we have those people who flip houses for the sake of seeing the final product when everything is said and done.

While none of the above reasons are better than the other, it is a matter of strategy. Flipping as a strategy doesn't suit everyone, but often works well for the following purposes:

- If you want to quit your nine-to-five job quickly. Developing a sizeable buy-to-let portfolio to substitute your income via rent would take many years, but you can run a couple of flip projects every year—the profits may then replace your salary.

- When you want to raise funds for "buy-to-let deposits". If you have enough deposit for a single property that is not sufficient for building a portfolio. Once you purchase one, you run out of cash and get stuck. If you use the money to flip a property, then the profit you make could be sufficient for a buy-to-let deposit—while you will still have your initial funds to flip again.

How Much Money Can You Make flipping Houses?

You may be wondering whether flipping houses generates a lot of money or it is merely hyped for no reason. Plus, what are your odds of being successful or failing?

Finding answers to the above questions is the first step in deciding whether flipping is the right choice for you.

What Is The Average Earning For A House Flipper?

When you consider the average income that flippers receive per house, you will know that the flipping business can earn you a huge amount of cash. For example, the gross profit for homes in the United States is around $29,342. While this is a significant profit, you have an opportunity to make more if you flip houses that command $100-200,000.

The state also determines the amount of money that house flippers can generate. For instance, house flippers from Massauchetts made a gross profit of about $103,384 per house in 2013, while flippers in California generated $99,999 per home in the same year.

While these figures represent the average earnings, it is possible for a house flipper to make even more or less. It depends on how skilled and talented a person is. However, it is good to know the chances of success or failure before getting started in this business.

How Successful Are Flippers?

In an ideal world, everyone would make a profit from this business. It would be a simple type of investment. However, the world is never perfect, and you need to commit your time and effort. As a result, not everyone achieves success from flipping houses.

For example, 40% of flipped houses do not return a profit. That should tell you that you aren't guaranteed to succeed in flipping business just because someone else is making a profit.

60% who succeed in house flipping share a few things. First, they have enough capital to pump into the business. Keep in mind that real estate investment is not that cheap, and you need to have some good starting capital. Even when you get a great deal on a foreclosed house, you still need to have some money to do some repairs in the house. You also need to have some extra funds on standby just in case you flip a house, and it fails to sell immediately.

They also have sufficient time to handle the project. You will need to allocate a few months into searching for a home to buy. Next, you need some weeks to repair, list, and finally sell it. As you can see, you need to have time to do all these tasks. If you can't find time to do this, the chances of not making it are high.

Another similarity between successful house flippers is that they like to do repairs early. Some do it by themselves, while others employ professionals.

Also, most house flippers are updated with the current news in real estate. They know when the market is right for them to sell houses and when not to sell. They have learned the tricks to use to assess the potential of a property. In other words, if you do not know how to analyze the market, you will end up buying a lemon that you cannot move.

That aside, patience is required. It is important not only in real estate but in any other form of investment. Patience is the rule of the game; if you run out of patience, you may get a bad offer. And no one wants to land a bad suggestion. By being patient, you will know the time to hold onto the property and when to sell it.

Similarly, the best house flippers don't quote a huge price for the property. They simply put it on sale at a fair price, making sure that they can get some profit. If you overprice a property, it can turn out to be the worst mistake. Why? The property may waste away on the market with no one wanting to buy it.

House flipping can be a risky business, but it is worth it if you make a profit from it. Take time to understand the best prices and then dive into the game. If you are ready, you can cash in one house after the next.

How Much Money Do You Need To Fix And Flip Houses? The Four Key Things To Consider

There are many things to consider when entering the market of house flipping.

Two of the most popular questions among newbies are: "What is the cost of flipping a house" and "Will a significant profit be made?".

The cost of flipping a home is equivalent to the total of the acquisition cost, carrying costs, sales costs, renovation costs, and marketing costs. The costs are different because it depends on the location of the home, the type of property, and the number of renovations that are supposed to be done. However, the total amount of money to flip a house is roughly 10% of the buying price.

How much you will spend to flip a home will vary from project to project. And that is one of the reasons why real estate is so exciting. Although the exact amount for a flip will be different, each project will often feature the four expenses.

The four major expenses of flipping a home include:

1. The buying price of a fix and flip property

Acquisition of property is defined as the amount of money that one will have to cash in to get a property. The costs associated with the purchase of a property comprise of the asking price of the house and the closing charges. Typically, the closing costs include the charges paid during the settlement of the transaction, and it includes the transfer fees, financing fees, and title insurance.

The buying price is the amount of cash you pay to get a property. The buying price is made up of the value of the land and the property built on the land. Another aspect of the purchase price is whether it is a multi-family home or single family. The buying price does not involve the insurance or taxes, but it depends on the way the deal is set—it might include appliances, light fixtures, and custom window treatments.

Before you buy a property, there are two essential factors that you need to pay attention to: comparing the prices of properties to understand how the properties are measured and sticking to the rule of thumb, where you pay "70% of the after repair value (ARV) of a property minus the rehab costs." If it's your first time in house flipping, then you should buy a property that requires only cosmetic repairs. And the reason why you are advised to do so is that it will be easy to figure out the costs. You can use the formula below to make sure that you get profitable deals and stay clear of money-pits:

Maximum Allowable Offer = (ARV x .70) – Repair Cost

This formula computes a 30% margin by taking into consideration critical costs: buying the property and performing repairs. It is a quick method to determine whether a deal is good for the home flipper.

Closing costs when buying a fix and flip home

When you purchase a house to flip, you should be ready to pay for some closing costs. Some of the costs include your share of the property, property insurances, transfer taxes, title insurance, and title company fees. If you are going to fund the purchase, the funding will include its costs at the time of closing. Both your lender and realtor will give you extensive details about the closing costs.

A rule of thumb states that the charges of closing a deal will be 5% of the purchase property. That means that if you buy a property for $300,000, then you should be ready to pay approximately 5% of $300,000. It gives you $15,000. Therefore, the $300,000 property will cost about $315,000. As a result, the following costs will affect your budget and ROI, so you should not forget to include them when determining how much it can cost to flip a property.

2. The cost to rehab a house

The charges for rehab refer to those related to renovating a property that you want to flip. These costs are different because it depends on the length of the rehab, the state of the property, and the cost of labor around the area where the property is purchased.

The types of rehab costs

Fix and flip material and labor costs

When you want to calculate the cost of materials that you will need to flip a property, you also need to include the transport or delivery cost and whether equipment requires an expert to come and install it. Some products will have to be special ordered, which extends the time and increases the costs of delivery.

Their prices of materials will differ depending on the project scope, but it generally falls into two groups:

• Building materials: The most popular materials comprise of hardware, lumber, and paint.

• Appliances: Common appliances include refrigerator, HVAC, and stove.

Labor depends on the amount of money contractors are going to ask for their effort and time in renovating your project. They will ask you for money to install all the items. Some charge on an hourly basis, but most charge per project. You will discuss with the contractor and finalize with a formal contract. Based on the time the rehab may take, different types of workers will be involved.

Some of the most popular laborers include:

• Landscaper

• Plumber

• Electrician

• General contractor

• Day laborer

• Painter

The length of property rehab is an essential factor when evaluating the cost of flipping a house. For starters, it is right to go for a property that requires only cosmetic repairs so that you can reduce your rehab costs and manage the project. Once you gain experience, you can then start to select the property that demands moderate repairs.

Cosmetic home repairs costs for a fix and flip

These repairs refer to minimal repairs or improvements that make the property look attractive. When done in the right way, they increase the value of the property. These repairs are done for a short period, which cuts down the carrying costs. Both materials and cost of labor are low, but the cost of acquisition is higher because the property is already in a far a better state than one that requires a complete rehab.

Cosmetic repairs comprise of:

- Patching walls and interior painting

- Replacing carpet

- Basic landscaping that includes planting flowers, cutting grass, and cleaning the entranceway

- Replacing cabinet hardware

- Painting cabinets to make them look appealing and attractive.

Moderate home repairs cost

These house repairs require significant repair to enhance the property and raise the value of the house. Because they are large projects, a professional contractor will be required to perform them, which is going to increase your cost of material and labor. The cost of acquisition will rise, and also increase the carrying costs.

Examples of moderate home repairs:

- Repairing the kitchen to add stone countertops, appliances, new flooring, and new light fixtures

- Adding exterior landscaping like shrubs to increase the curb appeal

- Renovating bathrooms using modern, matching plumbing fixtures, neutral-colored tiles, and new toilets

Detailed home repairs

These repairs are essential when a house needs a complete renovation. These kinds of repairs reduce the cost of property acquisition but increase the expenses on labor and material. Since these repairs require permits and contractors, it will increase your estimated time, and also increase your carrying costs.

Extensive house repairs comprise:

- Adding another room

- Adding a garage

- Fixing problems such as cracks in the foundation

- Construct a new bathroom

The example below shows how extensive house repairs may affect your ROI:

Assume that you have purchased a house for $100,000 and then spend $25,000 on doing cosmetic maintenance. Now the current value of the home is $155,000 (this doesn't include the carrying costs or closing costs). In other words, the ROI for the following project is going to be: $30,000/$125,000 x 100 = 24%.

3. Carrying costs for property flipping

These refer to the repeated expenses that you will spend now and then to buy a house until the day you flip it. In general, you pay this cost at the end of the month once the property becomes yours.

The most common type of carrying costs is financing, but there are also other costs such as insurance, property taxes, and utilities.

Financing costs

These costs are associated with borrowing cash to purchase and enhance a home. For example, a house flipper can use a private loan to buy a home. They can then use the credit card to finance the costs of repair.

Average fix and flip lenders will offer a significant interest rate for a short period. However, you can use a mortgage calculator to find an estimated number. Keep in mind that there are different types of flip lenders, and you need to make some comparisons first.

Home-style repair loans and hard money lenders charge a financing fee in different ways.

Hard money loan for fix and flip

Hard money lenders, as the name suggests, will lend cash to investors. This loan is often released by private firms to facilitate a short financing timeline.

Some of the costs associated with this type of loan include points paid during closing. The borrower can also cut some of the appraisal fee. This fee is specific to professionals to help them complete a written approximation of the market value of the property. Keep in mind that each lender has their requirements.

Home-style renovation loan for fix and flip

For the home-style renovation loan, it will include the costs for the renovation and the buying price of the house. This loan will allow borrowers to buy a house that requires some repair.

A property qualifies for a home-style renovation loan if the renovations are permanent and increase the value of the property. A 15-30 year fixed rate plus adjustable mortgage rates are provided. The lender has to approve the contractors doing the renovations.

The all Cash financing

Another option for financing a house is all cash. This one will save you money in a short period because there is no interest, fees or points. However, using all the cash to buy a property means that you use money that you could channel into something else, and you will not have the leverage to buy multiple homes.

When you used this option, you must have the cash to buy a property and the money to perform repairs. Besides this, you will need to have some funds at your disposal to account for unexpected costs. Another external expense will involve the carrying costs.

The property tax cost to flip a house

The house taxes will determine the cost to fix and flip a home in two ways. First, at the time of the agreement, you may need to pay the rest of the taxes. Another way is that there could be monthly taxes for the property.

In the US, property tax rates are different because of the varying amount of taxes set by states. For example, properties separated by blocks may have different taxes. A hefty tax burden placed on homes can chase away home buyers. You need to consider this when flipping because you want your renovated home to attract many home buyers.

Costs of insurance

Insurance of property is a type of policy that guarantees financial compensation to homeowners in case their property or its contents are destroyed. Coverage is also vital to secure you, and the owner of the property, from possible litigation. Examples of property insurance types consist of flood, fire, and hazard. A house flipper will possibly require vacant house insurance, which is a bit different from a homeowner's policy.

This one will cover the property at the time of the flip, in case it is destroyed, or suffers destruction from a storm. You can choose to pay upfront, before settlement, or monthly. This insurance cost will differ depending on where the property is located, the expected timeline of vacancy, and the value of the property.

Utility cost

The forms of utility cost that are important to house flippers include electric gas, water, and oil. The following charges have to be included in the "monthly carrying costs".

Utility bills differ depending on the property condition, size, and usage. You can get in touch with the previous owner to calculate the monthly estimate. When you buy a home, the utility providers can spend some weeks before they start to provide you with the services, so you should alert them immediately. It is impossible for contractors to carry our renovations without electricity and water. If they get stuck, it will eat much of your money and increase your time.

4. Fix and flip marketing and cost of sales

When you involve a realtor, the majority of the costs for selling and marketing a property will include out-of-pocket expenses but will originate from proceeds of the settlement. But when you sell the property by yourself and decide not to involve a realtor, you will need to pay for the upfront marketing costs.

The above marketing and sale costs will involve realtor fees, closing costs, and marketing costs.

The three types of fix and flip sales costs and marketing costs comprise:

The fees of the realtor when flipping a house

It is the responsibility of the seller to pay for realtor fees. The following fees will include a commission from both realtors if two realtors are involved. In general, one realtor will represent the seller, and the other one will represent the buyer. The standard fees of a realtor are 6%, but it can include any amount that both the seller and realtor agree on.

The realtor fees comprise of sale costs and marketing costs. That represents the most significant percentage of the closing costs that a seller should be responsible. In case the subject property is about $200,000, then the fees for the realtor will be $12,000. These are not an out-of-pocket expense, but they are reduced from the sales price of the house during settlement.

The marketing costs required to flip a house

The costs of marketing are low when you use a realtor to sell your fix and flip property. In case you sell a property yourself, then these costs will rise, and it will have to be paid out of pocket. The cost of marketing comprises of online postings, flyers, open house expenses, and for sale signs.

The above costs are usually ignored when computing the carrying costs. However, they are critical in receiving positive exposure for the house. The property is advertised to more prospective buyers, and the chances of one buyer purchasing the property are high. This will then reduce the carrying costs.

The costs of marketing a flip house differ depending on the approach of buying and the skills of the investor.

House flipping selling and closing costs

A closing cost is a fee that is released at the time of closing in a real estate transaction. This happens when the title of the property is delivered to the buyer. There is no upfront paid, but it is deducted from the sales price of the property. Most of the seller's closing costs originate from the fees of the realtor.

Another closing cost that the seller has to pay is any outstanding taxes of the house and utilities, transfer taxes, and any credits that the seller sends the buyer. Averagely, the closing costs can be equivalent to approximately 2% to 5% of the sales price of the property.

Calculating how much it can cost to flip a house

First, you need to begin with the possible ARV and work backward to prevent all the four significant costs in line. In case you know the price of the property before you buy it, you will be able to tell the budget for the rehab costs, and the budget for carrying costs, sales, and marketing.

You can calculate the costs to flip a property by using the following factors:

The ARV for flipping a house

Once the repair value is complete, next is an approximation of what the property will be worth once the proposed repairs are over. You can estimate the ARV for your property by comparing properties that have been sold recently within the same neighborhood as the property you want to buy. The comparison should involve properties identical to what the renovated property will be.

ARV is an excellent tool because it provides a rough estimate before presenting an offer. That will include the rehab costs, carrying costs, and if possible, compute the numbers during every transaction—you will not overpay for a house. ARV impacts your ROI—the less you pay for a property, the more profit you will generate.

The budget to flip a house

A budget refers to a summary of the estimated costs for a given period. When you purchase a flipped house, the budget will include your rehab expenses, carrying costs, and property acquisition costs.

The budget is very critical when you are determining the cost needed to flip a property. It will ensure that you are in line with your contractors and the cost of the material. It will also be a vital tool to ensure that you monitor money spent and note where too much is spent. By sticking to the budget, you will achieve your expected ROI, and your fix and flip will be profitable.

Fix and flip timeline

A timeline details the time expected for a fix and flip process to happen. It will be set at the start of the project or course of the project. The timeline begins immediately when you buy a property and comes to an end when you sell the property.

For instance, you can set a timeline of 60 days from the day you buy the property to when you expect to sell it. The timeline has to involve the following things:

- The size of the property
- Marketing and selling of the property
- The scope of the rehab work
- Schedule and availability
- Contractor's availability

Keep in mind that the timeline is critical, just like the budget. The shorter the timeline, the less expensive the carrying costs will be. In other words, your projected ROI will be okay, and the profit will be higher. Conversely, if the timeline extends past the goal, then your carrying costs will rise, and your ROI will reduce.

The projected return on investment

The projected ROI is the amount of money you expect to get when you sell a flipped house. A high ROI means high profit, which is the purpose of committing time and money on the project. The lower the ROI, the lower your profit. The budget, ARV, and timeline will impact your ROI. The formula for determining ROI include:

ROI = Net profit/Total investment x 100

For instance, if your net profit is equal to $40,000, then your total investment is $200,000. So this translates to a 20% ROI.

Frequently Asked Questions About The Cost To Flip A House

What is the average return on investment when you flip a property?

The average ROI for a flipped house is between 10-20%. However, ROI will vary depending on the type of house being flipped. Other factors that will affect the ROI include sales costs, timeline, rehab costs, and acquisition cost. In general, the shorter your timeline, the higher your ROI. Just remember that each decision you make while flipping a house will affect your ROI. Just learn to stick to your budget and ensure that your costs are as low as possible.

How long can it take to flip a house?

The timeline for flipping a house varies because of a few things. Some factors that affect the timeline are the degree of exposure of the flipper, the length of rehab needed, type of financing used, size of the property, and the local real estate market.

On average, it can take 90 days for experienced flippers to buy, repair, and sell a house. Remember that extensive properties and the ones that require a lot of rehabs may take longer than expected.

How much can it cost to rehab a house?

There is no fixed answer to this question because it depends on the number of repairs needed, the size of the house, the cost of acquisition, timeline, and the location of the house. If a property is found in an area where building materials and labor is costly, then you should be ready for a big budget.

In general, the costs of rehab may be around 10% of the buying price of the house. That means if you buy a house for $400,000, you should be ready to spend approximately $40,000 on rehab.

The main point is that the cost of flipping a house changes depending on several factors, including rehab costs, financing costs, acquisition costs, and carrying costs. The average expense of flipping a house is determined by computing 10% of the buying price. By taking into consideration each of the mentioned factors, you should be on the right track to knowing how much you need to have to flip a house.

How to analyze markets like experts?

In this section, you will learn the four necessary steps you can use to evaluate house flipping deals to ensure that you make the highest profit.

Mastering how to analyze a deal will be the first step to success in flipping houses. However, very few people in real estate ever learn this vital skill. Whether you like it or not, after reading this section, you will perhaps know much about this technique—even better so than investors or realtors.

You can find all the properties in the world, but until you learn how to evaluate them and create good offers accurately, it won't be of any benefit. Learning how to assess properties and generate the best offers is the secret to making a profit from flipping houses.

If you decide to watch any TV shows that discuss house flipping, you will rarely learn how to evaluate a property. They exclude most costs that can cause huge problems if you ignore them at the start of your property analysis.

So by learning this principle, it will set you aside from a "speculator" who just buys a house because they hope that it will increase in value until it attains the heights of a true "investor", someone who is aware of the costs involved in real estate and doesn't depend on guesswork. The true investor includes the calculated risks and precisely knows how to make a major profit on their investment.

All right! Let's get started.

This section is divided into four critical steps to help you learn how to make offers that will always ensure that you earn a profit from every transaction:

1. Compute the ARV

ARV stands for "After Repaired Value". It is a common phrase among investors in real estate. As the name suggests, ARV is the value of the property once the renovation is complete. Determining the cost of a property once you are done with repairs is always the first thing when evaluating a deal. If you can't identify the ARV, then it's just difficult to proceed because you have no ground to start from.

For you to precisely compute the ARV, then you will have to consider the "comparables or comps". These are properties that have been sold recently or are up for sale. The properties resemble yours and are in the same locality as your property. Use the "comparables" to calculate the "going rate" for homes in that locality—this is a great sign to show what your house will cost.

If you want to find information or data for "comparable properties", you can opt for free or paid services from Zillow. However, if you are interested in comprehensive information, you will have to consider Multiple Listing Service (MLS). This one will provide detailed information about each property that is put on sale or has recently been sold.

To use MLS, you will need to look for an agent or work with someone who has permission to log in to the MLS.

The first thing after you log in to the MLS is to search for repaired "standard" sold comparables similar to what your home will appear when all renovations are complete. These kind of properties are easy to identify. You will notice that some have great pictures, and look more attractive than other homes. These are the houses that you should put a lot of emphasis on when calculating your ARV.

Next, based on the number of "standard" sold comps you get, you might want to include other recently sold homes which are in good condition or have been renovated.

As a rule of thumb, search for homes that have the following characteristics:

- They have been sold in the last 90-120 days:

- The distance between the homes is half to three-quarters of a mile from your property.

- They are in the same neighborhood as your property.

Once you finish searching at the recently sold properties, then you can now extend your hunt to properties that are pending because they are under contract with a buyer, and are yet to close.

Pending properties are important because it will allow you to get an idea of the projected future values—but keep in mind that these may not sell for the set price.

Avoid crossing the tracks

Don't use properties from a separate city, school, or district. Additionally, pay attention to garage sizes, views, swimming pools, and any other upgrade so that you can set a fair value.

Lastly, you can also include the latest trends in the market, and seasonal changes in price for signs on the resell value of your house and the right time to sell or buy.

As you can see, there are many things that you need to remember when calculating your ARV. While there is no precise formula for determining the ARV, keep in mind that it can sometimes be challenging.

2. Estimate the cost of repairs

Now that you have determined your ARV, the next thing is to accurately come up with a proposal price to approximate the expense of repairs. With time, you will become so good at this that you will be able to estimate the cost of repair by only looking at pictures or having a description, and being aware of the age and size of the property within 1-2% without even setting your eyes on it. That means that with some time and a bit of experience, estimating repairs won't be a difficult task.

The "$20 per sq ft" rule is a great hint regarding the cost to fix a property. Briefly, this rule originates from the idea that most properties that need a complete "standard" cosmetic repair will cost about "$20 per square foot".

In other words, if you are planning on purchasing a property that is about 1,500 sq ft, you can estimate to spend about $30,000 for renovation (1,500 x $20).

However, this rule is based on the assumption that you are renovating a mid-entry or entry property. So if you are going to rehab a much better house and using advanced materials, then you may need to change the rate and use something like "$25 or $35 per square foot". However, for the standard basic repair, the "$20 per sq ft" rule works pretty well.

From here, you can either move it up or down depending on the extra requirements or things you don't want. For instance, if you would like to replace the roof, then you may need to include $6,000-$9,000.

After some time, you will have a precise knowledge of these costs, and you will be able to determine the rehab costs without much effort.

Remember that you will only use the $20 per sq ft formula when you come up with the initial price offer. Once your offer is accepted, you will perhaps want to evaluate the property with a professional contractor and develop a comprehensive scope of work and renovation estimates to make sure that you don't miss anything with your first estimate.

You can do this on your own or "wholesale" the house to a different investor—you can also meet with them, and if they are professionals, they can pay you a fee and purchase the home.

3. Determine the cost for closing and holding expenses

This is an area that is often forgotten in most house flipping shows. Flipping houses can be stressful if all the money that you make sinks into costs.

Below we look at some of the expenses that you must know when calculating your offer for property investment:

Purchase closing costs

These involve the closing expenses that you spend when you purchase a house. In the past, the seller is responsible for paying the closing costs, so when you buy a house, your costs will essentially be lower than when you sell the property.

Selling costs

At this point, things can be a little hard. If you are going to involve an agent, then you must be ready to pay a specific commission. Depending on the place and market, your buyer can request for concessions to help you pay the costs.

Based on the location and market, your buyer can ask for concessions to help pay for their costs. This can be between 1-6%, but it is usually 3%.

Holding costs

Holding costs is another type of cost that most people forget to consider when planning to buy an investment property. Holding costs may comprise of utilities, maintenance, insurance, and taxes.

Financing costs

If you are going to use your capital, then you need not fear the costs of financing, but if you don't have enough money and you have to follow the path that most people do when financing, then be sure to account for that.

If you plan to use a private lender, you should be ready to pay between 8-12% of your capital. If you are going to involve a hard money lender in the current market, then you should be prepared to pay approximately 12% of the additional points and fees.

Most lenders of hard money will charge between two-three points, but this is not annualized, so no matter how long you decide to borrow the cash, this is what you are going to pay on the cash you borrow. The charges will differ, but you may be required to determine for an extra "point," or an additional 1%, for the above expenses.

That means if you plan to pay a private lender 12%, that will be equal to 1% each month you borrow the cash. If you plan to hold the money for four months, then you will need to calculate for 4%.

4. Determine your offer

Once you develop the right method of computing your potential selling price, and you can estimate the possible costs, then it is the right time to come up with the price offer.

There are different formulas that you can use to determine what to offer on a specific property.

Formula 1:

(ARV) – (Repair Costs) – (Closing and Holding Costs) – (Desired pr

This is the most basic formula, and perhaps the most accurate means to determine your price offer.

It narrows down to finding out what you can sell the property for and subtracting all your costs and expected profit. And then you get your price offer.

Your expected profit will, of course, be determined by how much you want to make. Perhaps you will have to leave some room for error, but you will discover that if you go too low on your offers, the chances of purchasing many houses are going to be low.

For most cases, it is better to ensure that your profit involves a % contrary to just a number. It has to do with managing returns on capital, risk, and the bigger picture. As quick advice when getting started, you can compute 10% of your ARV for the profit. Therefore, if the ARV is about $250,000, then the profit will be $25,000.

Formula 2:

ARV x 70% – Repair Costs = Offer Price

This formula is also known as the "70% rule".

From this formula, you select what the property should sell for and minus the costs of repair, and then you set aside 30% to account for holding and closing costs.

Here is an example:

Assume a fixed up house is $200,000 and the costs of repair account for $25,000, then this is how you should determine your offer:

$200,000 (ARV) x 70% – $25,000

(Repairs) = **$115,000**

That looks simple, right?

However, one thing you need to know is that this is not a formula to just fit in values, but you need to adjust some things depending on the project scope, timeline, market conditions, and the means of financing.

Sometimes this formula is used with 60%, 80% or even 90%. But if you are just getting started, you can be safe by applying the 70% rule and then changing it from there.

So far, you have learned some great ideas on how to calculate the ARV of a property, you know how to estimate repairs, and you know what to expect for closing or holding costs. You have even learned some great formulas to help you determine your deals.

At first, you will feel overwhelmed, but no one said flipping houses is as easy as one, two, three, and if anyone has told you that, then they are dreaming!

Finding, Managing And Paying Contractors

For anyone who has attempted to recruit a contractor or even a handyman to come and do some repairs on their business or home, you probably know how difficult it can be to find the best contractor. So why is it so difficult?

There are two main reasons:

> 1. Contractors aren't good business owners. This issue is part of the "E-myth" mentality, which states that because a person knows how to bake, they can run a bakery. Or just because someone knows how to swing a hammer, they can respond to a phone call on time!

2. Real estate investors will be looking for a great deal, which means they don't involve the "big guys"—those who are experienced at running their business— because they know they will be too costly.

So what can an investor do? How can they add a contractor to their "team"?

A great contractor who can convert your house from a state of unlivable to "ready to sell" will be important in your house flipping business.

Unfortunately, there are scary narratives about wrong contractors resulting in huge delays and headaches. Thus, this section will look at some methods to use to find the best contractors to ensure your house flipping investment runs smoothly.

First, which places can you find contractors? Below are some options that have been found to work:

1. REIC referrals

You can start by visiting your local Real Estate Investment Club. The investors who come to attend the following meetings will possibly have some referrals for you to look for. And because you can be sure that they have worked with them before, you know that the contractors will have an excellent track record. These kinds of connections can be beneficial.

2. Farm area

Another means to get contractors is by walking around your "farm area" and searching for contractors. Get closer and start a conversation. You will get the opportunity to see how they do their work and the kind of work they do in a real-life environment.

3. Hardware stores

You can also look for contractors near your local Home Depot. You should try to show up early so you can be sure that you will be working alongside a person with a professional work history. It is easy to identify them because they are the ones who are buying a considerable amount of house-rehabbing supplies.

4. Search online

No need to oversimplify this: search for a local contractor online. Get in touch with them over the phone and find out how you rate them. Ask them to provide you with references and request permission to see their projects. However, keep in mind that merely because you are calling them, doesn't imply that you have to give them the job.

The rule of 3

If you are getting started in the house flipping business, the Rule of 3 is the best tool to assist you any time you want to hire a contractor.

When about to hire contractors, focus on starting with three different contractors to provide you with your estimates. By the time you finish meeting each of them and know something about their perspective, you will be surprised at how much you have learned.

Quick tip

Once you are familiar with the expense for rehabs, then you can send questions to prospective contractors concerning their fee structure. Here is a quick secret that you can always use when searching for a contractor:

Just ask them to tell you how much they want to be paid for painting the interior of a "1500 sq ft" house plus the ceilings.

Now, if they quote you the "best" price, they should be ready to do it for $1 per sq ft. That means if they say a rough figure of about $3,000, then you can tell that they are not the best contractor because they don't know the correct value when working with real estate investors and striking a repeat business.

And thus you have saved a great deal of time.

Sub Or Not To Sub?

There are various schools of thought that encourage one to either employ subcontractors and manage them on their own, or not. However, it is better to work with a general contractor. If you hire the right general contractor, they will learn how to work and manage their people, so you will directly be working with them and paying only a single contractor. And when you find the right general contractor, not only will they know how to take care of your whole project but they can control different projects at once. There is nothing more terrible than trying to control and pay different contractors at the same time.

Even when your project demands that you hire a subcontractor, bring a general contractor to handle the project. It will save you a lot of time.

Systems And Materials

It may take time, but after the first two rehabs, you need to compile a list of all fixtures, colors, and SKU numbers for different rehab materials you use. That will be your price sheet. After some time, you switch an item with something that performs better, but in most cases, you need to have a list of products that your contractor is going to use on each project rehab.

There could be periods when a house does not require new countertops or something else, so remove those from the list. But in most cases, it saves a lot of time and energy when planning a rehab.

The Discussion

Like in any form of negotiation, when negotiating a project with a contractor, your focus should be a win-win situation.

After all, you want to build a house flipping business. You need to purchase properties at a discount, renovate them at a cost-friendly price, and finally sell them for a profit. It is critical to consider that contractors perhaps spend roughly half of their time promoting themselves. They tend to spend many hours looking for jobs to bid on, bidding on the tasks and not winning most of their bids.

So the goal is for them to know that you are not a "retail" client; your purpose is to work with a contractor with whom you can shift to different projects. By doing so, they do not have to spend many hours searching for jobs to bid. If you can help them have some peace of mind by making them know that they will always have work, then they don't need to waste their time bidding.

Just A Reminder

Always verify that you are working with a professional contractor who is insured and licensed. It is highly advised that you come up with a price sheet that demonstrates how you will pay on a sq ft basis.

When you have these "pre-agreed" standard items, it will save you a great deal of time during negotiation. You will work with different contractors, but the best ones will remain at the top. So let them exactly know what you want, and you will both be happy at the end of the project.

Remote Investing

It is rare to look beyond where you stay when searching for your next investment. The probability of your local area generating that kind of growth is very small. And with technology improving, it has never been easier to look beyond the field.

Not all real estate investment markets are the same, and where you decide to invest your hard earned money can be the difference in your ROI. Many people turn on the neighborhood for real estate investing but could be looking at other markets to generate higher cap rates and create diversity in their portfolio.

Remote real estate investment is an area of debate among investors. One side supports the idea of freedom they found when they decided to invest in places far from where they stay, while others reject this. They consider it a risky venture.

So Who Is Right?

Should you decide to invest away from your state? Is remote real estate investment profitable? Is it okay for you or you should maintain your local investment? In real estate, location is a significant factor that will determine how much profit you can make.

And if where you choose to invest is important, the remote versus local discussion should perhaps spread more than it is now.

What Is Remote Investing?

Remote investing is a simple real estate investment technique where you decide to invest in strong markets outside the U.S. This means that you own income properties in these markets and collaborate with a partner to supervise the day-to-day management.

Myths About Investing Remotely In Real Estate

The primary thing that prevents real estate investors from attempting to invest remotely is the fear of the unknown. Some of the concern have some truths, while others appear less true based on the way you invest and the degree of due diligence applied.

Investing Remotely Is Expensive

It is not always as true as most investors think. But why do people say so? Because you will need to outsource everything when you decide to invest remotely. Since you are far from the place, you have to hire a landlord to work on your behalf. You need to look for a property management team, and finding the right person to do it is by all means very expensive.

Alternatively, finding a company that can handle all the responsibilities for you is a significant investment, especially if you plan to build your portfolio in the location with the management team.

Not only this, but it is also a bit expensive because of the differences in the cost of living and prices across the country. So one of the primary reasons that cause investors to turn to remote investing is because the local market does not generate a profitable investment.

Chapter 3: Property Wholesaling

Real estate wholesaling is the best real estate type of investment method. However, before you can achieve success as a real estate wholesaler, you need to understand the ins and outs of it. Before diving into details, it is essential to know what commercial real estate investing is. When we talk about real estate wholesaling, then it means that your role is the middleman: you get a motivated seller, discuss the property for a specific low price, and then resell the property for a low price but higher than the initial estimate. The difference between the two prices is your profit.

Why Real Estate?

If you hold a mortgage, then you are investing in real estate, and this means that you are a real estate investor. There are many reasons why you need to be involved in real estate transaction and have your property.

Everyone has different reasons why they want to invest in real estate. Your intentions are a motivating factor in choosing your business model, but there is at least something for everyone.

If you are searching for long-term financial freedom, then it will make sense to create your rental portfolio so that you can receive cash flow every month.

For those who are not interested in working much and may want to spend their time traveling, turnkey rentals or wholesaling can be great options.

Individuals who are looking to manage and work in rehab can make huge profits in the short-run through fix-n-flip projects.

With various exit strategies comes different benefits to take advantage of. However, not all benefits can apply for each exit strategy.

For that reason, if you are stuck and you don't know whether to invest in real estate, here are some reasons that should help you make up your mind:

1. Real estate has money flowing for many centuries

Generating income by owning land and property has been a common trend for centuries. Feudalism was a mix of legal and martial customs during Medieval Europe that expanded between the ninth and fifteenth centuries. It was a system that organized society based on the relationships in terms of holding land in exchange for service and labor roles.

Not much has changed since that time. Renting out real estate is one of the oldest types of business. In the past, the nobility owned extensive territory; the overclass controlled the underclass. Today, even if the wealthy have vast land and property, it is a different story, whereby anyone can own land and property if they have enough capital.

2. Appreciation

Most of the products you purchase often depreciate as time goes by. However, real estate is one of the few things that you can be sure will appreciate the longer you continue to own it. And this is the reason why rental properties are a great option because you will most likely have a plan to maintain it for a specific number of years.

While the market experiences various cycles, the real estate boasts of a steady appreciation over time. There is a constant rise in demand for rental properties in the US, and with this demand, prices increase.

In other words, as long as you purchase the correct price and in the right location, you should sit back and see how the value of the property increases over time for a rental property. The additional benefit of your renter's paying can generate a great percentage of profit over some time.

3. Cash flow on rentals

Rental properties are the best long-term investment option. With a rental property, typically, you will be making a profit every month in cash flow per property, which begins to add up as you develop your rental portfolio.

When you have rental properties, you will have tenants pay the mortgage and pay enough to cover your "added expenses," and you will remain with lots of profit.

Investing in a single rental property will not cause massive damage to your financial freedom, but it will generate money every month as long as someone is living in the property.

With a rental investment, the more you own, the better. If you want to narrow down the number of rentals you have, it is vital to create a property management company to deal with the day-to-day operations. This way, it is more passive, and you can focus on getting more deals.

4. You gain control

You become your boss when you are a real estate investor. You have the option to build a customized business for your lifestyle. Hate the idea of working on Fridays? Don't worry.

Do you want to try a new marketing approach this month? Sure!

Do you want to work while lazing at the beach? Go for it.

It is good to concentrate on your goals and what your "why" is so that you can know what to work hard for. By doing this, you will learn how to reverse engineer whatever you need to do every month so that you are on target to fulfill your goals.

If you want to generate a certain amount of income every month, then you can perform the calculations to determine the number of deals and the amount of profit that you need. Don't forget to count in any closing costs, advertising, and rehab for this.

5. Principal pay down

This also applies to real estate business, but it is important because it solidifies the cash flow. With the principal paydown, as long as you have a tenant occupying the property, your mortgage payment will be paid for you. As time goes by, your mortgage can even be paid off, purely from tenants who pay their rent. After this, your monthly cash flow will rise very fast.

6. Tax benefits

Tax benefits differ depending on your exit plan. You have depreciation, possibly tax-free cash flow, the ability to perform a 101 exchange and much more. There are write-offs for interest paid on property and extra expenses involved in a rental property.

While we are not tax advisors, you need to keep a close watch on your tax benefits. It is critical to get in touch with an investor-friendly advisor to ensure that you take advantage of all the tax benefits that you can apply.

7. The leverage of other money

Most investors in real estate don't use their cash to pay for a deal in full. Most can do this, but they don't have to, and it will allow them to narrow their business faster if they include other people's money.

Why is this so?

When an investor has $100,000 in cash reserves and concentrates it on one-two deals, then they will be restricted to wait until the deals get buyers and close before having the cash to use again.

If you use a loan from a lender, you may put $10,000 into the deal of your money and make use of the credit for the remaining payment. You will pay the interest for a short interval and reap the profit from the deal.

Based on your exit strategy, you may not require a long-term loan and don't even mind paying interest because it will provide you with leverage to do many deals.

8. Positive change in the economy

At one point, we need some good karma. When purchasing a distressed house or vacant home to renovate it, you will be improving the neighborhood. Most of the properties that investors are searching for are those that would not be immediately for sale in the market because they require a lot of work to be rehabbed, and it is hard to finance them through traditional lenders. Some property investors who stay outside the state fail to commit the right care needed for each property.

Most neighbors don't want to stay close to a deteriorating property because it can negatively affect the value of properties around it.

When purchasing an investment property, you will be in one way or another enhancing the quality of the neighborhood.

9. Huge profit opportunity

Hitting rental estate property with a lucrative deal is what everyone strives for, but even a few of the mid-range deals will generate a decent profit.

However, not every deal will generate tens of thousands of dollars, but in general, you have the probability of creating a nice payday if you know how to correctly analyze a deal and offer a price that generates a profit when you sell. Rehabs usually have the best return on investment, but you should not ignore other exit strategies.

Cycles Of Real Estate

With most things happening in life, the best thing that someone can tell you is to give yourself a break and think about the big picture. However, when you are assessing the rental markets for investment, you will realize that you need to get into the little details.

By deriving assumptions from your local market to another, then you run the risk of overs implying the market and ignoring possible deals that can generate substantial cash flow. Remember that markets can be in different phases at the same time. Look at it like the weather: just because it is raining in New York does not imply that there can't be sunshine in Washington at the same time.

Understanding real estate markets, including the little details, and being able to identify the phase every market is going through at a particular moment, is the primary tool for detecting a good or bad investment.

Successful real estate investors keep a close look on the real estate cycle to recognize investment opportunities. Just like the bigger economy, there are four types of real estate phases:

- Expansion
- Recession
- Recovery
- Hyper supply

The cycle repeats in waves so that the last recession of the cycle generates the recovery period of the next cycle. As an investor, you should use the real estate cycle to measure your investment plan. However, it is hard to know how long each cycle will last.

What does the real estate cycle speak to investors?

When you take a close look at the current real estate phase, it can reveal much about the desirability of an investment chance. Finding out whether you are in the recovery, hyper supply, expansion, or recession phase will allow you to make assumptions about the amount of return you can expect on your investment. You can also make a correct guess of how long you will need to hold the property and what your exit strategy will be. The real estate cycle can show the income and appreciation performance of a specific property, and it can tell the best time to make capital improvements.

1. Recovery phase

The recovery phase is the most challenging phase to detect. When a rental market is in the process of recovery from the recession, the demand can be very slow. The growth of rental income can appear flat. But to those who are closely monitoring the data, the upward trend in property listings and the reduced speed of the previous decline in the downward direction are all signs that the market is headed in a downturn.

At the time of recovery, the value-add properties that require renovation demand careful analysis but can provide an opportunity to improve, acquire, and then resell the asset for better returns during the incoming phase of expansion. That will also be the time to enhance significant assets in an attractive location and ride the market up to development.

2. Expansion

The markets in expansion phase are in the process of transitioning and encountering with increasing demand. The growth of jobs in the following markets will appear sharp, rents will rise, and vacancy will be low. New construction jobs are important, and at the height of the following phase, both the supply and demand attain equilibrium.

During this period, developers can take advantage of the increased demand.

It is also the right time to apply value-add tactics. Investors who know what they are searching for can look for a safe neglected property that needs TLC, then turn these assets into full productivity before they can resell for a specific profit.

3. Hyper Supply

Hyper supply happens when the economy starts to decline or new developments progress in parallel with the falling demand. Both affect the occupancy rates and slow down the rental growth.

During this phase, smart investors search for stable tenants and long leases that are in place. While no one can project the time when the next phase of expansion will occur, these fixed-term assets make sure that a certain degree of high performance is present until the next lease is released. Alternatively, investors that can maintain an even keel can utilize the gains of a prime real estate "divestitures" from overly worried sellers.

4. Recession

When the parties in the market do not want to identify the downturn or decide to ignore the cautionary signs of a warning plea, the hyper supply phase can fall into the recession phase. A recession is distinguished by its heavy supply, reductions in rent, and high vacancy rates. In the following high saturated market, investors that want to take on a high risk can look for distressed bank-owned homes, empty land developments, and construction projects at a friendly price. This is a long-term option for the patient investor ready to work to improve the asset and hold it until the time when the cycle moves back through the recovery phase. Investors have to be selective or risk being caught when they catch a falling knife.

Final Takeaway

The most important thing to remember is that markets can be in different cycles at the same time. Therefore, a plan that works in the hyper supply phase in New York will be less operational in the recession phase in California.

Besides this, it is difficult to predict the length of time each phase can last. Even if we consider the historical data, it is hard to base on the same highs and lows because the economy is dynamic. Also, the cycles can be different based on the geography and asset class; the goal is to remain vigilant and learn the nuances of every market and the right strategy to implement each scenario. By doing so, you can establish a diversified real estate investment portfolio strong enough to prevent any storm.

Tips To Match Your Strategy To The cycle

Remember that the four real estate cycles do not happen in equal periods. The recovery can be short and transition fast to expansion, or it might last for years. The real estate cycle also changes based on geographic and asset class factors. Savvy investors try to balance the performance of highs and lows using a different portfolio of investment concentrating on different methods.

What Everyone Should Know About Real Estate Investing

If you are interested in becoming a successful real estate investor, then you should perhaps begin by learning everything that you need to be aware of in real estate investing.

When we talk about "everything", it does not necessarily mean the initial details of each feature but the different features themselves.

There are a few crucial insights that everyone who wants to invest in real estate should be aware of—learning everything demands that you know what three aspects before digging deep into learning about every feature in detail.

Nowadays, everyone you meet seems to be an expert on real estate investing. Although it is true that real estate has made many Americans rich, this doesn't imply that everyone knows how to make massive profits in real estate or even run a real estate business. This section has broken down the list into five significant aspects, and what is it that you need to know to make the best investment choices and succeed as a real estate investor:

Appreciation

Appreciation refers to the rise in the value of real estate property after a certain period because of different factors, such as the growth and development of the area, or the performance of the real estate market as a whole.

While most starters in real estate believe that they can invest in real estate for appreciation, it is essential to understand that real estate investing appreciation is just icing on the cake.

Appreciation is something difficult to predict, and planning an investment around it can be a risky approach. Thus, when about to invest in real estate, exclude appreciation from the mix, and plan for the profits that you can generate without appreciation. In case appreciation does happen, then you will be generating extra profit that can be significant. However, do not invest in real estate because of appreciation—that is something that you should never forget.

Investment strategies

One of the first things that you should pay attention to when it comes to everything you should know about real estate investing is that there are different investment strategies that you can apply.

The investment strategies that exist in the real estate business are many and differ from each other. There are traditional investment strategies that have been in existence since the start of real estate investment; for example, the conventional rental strategy or the fix-and-flip strategy.

There are also other modern strategies of investment that you can apply; such as the rent-to-own strategy and lease option.

It is vital that you learn about the different investment strategies to identify one that is suitable for you and one that you can use to generate profits and in the amount of time you would like.

The Math

What this means is that you need to know the different metrics used to assess an investment property and determine its viability and expected profit—this should also include the way to compute the parameters and what it means.

You are perhaps familiar with the return on investment. What you may not be aware of is that real estate investment has numerous methods to help you determine the ROI. Besides, each technique has a unique application and advantages. All this depends on the type of investment strategy that you select or the type of property that you invest in.

Some of the most popular metrics in the real estate business include the cash on return and the cap rate. Both of the following metrics determine the ROI by using unique information about your investment property.

Laws and taxes

Laws and taxes have a crucial role in real estate investing, and it will determine all the features of your investment.

Besides, the biggest risk of investing in real estate is the lack of education or knowledge about the taxes and laws that affect your investment. In most cases, failure to understand the taxes or laws that apply to your real estate investment can cause serious issues that may lead to you losing property and all the money on your investment.

The best method for you to ensure that you know all the laws and taxes that affect your investment is to look for a tax expert or legal advisor. These are professionals that will guide you to understand the different rules and regulations.

Financing

You know that investing in real estate requires a person to have a large sum of money to buy property and perform repairs and renovations.

You may wonder how everyone seems to have all the money required to run a real estate venture. However, most people who invest in real estate do not use their money to buy property but borrow the cash from a lender. Once you arrive at the point where you are searching for a means to finance the purchase, you should know the options that you have to fund your investment.

There are a wide variety of loans and mortgages that are accessible to real estate investors. Each has its advantages and disadvantages, with some designed for specific investment strategies.

By understanding your options, it will allow you to create a better plan for your investment and all the features associated with it with the least amount of risk. This will also help you to discover more about the possible profits that you can generate from property investing.

The bottom line is that real estate investing is so much more than just buying a property and waiting for its value to rise.

Everything that you need to be aware of about real estate investment must be learned before you think about investing—after you have learned about each feature, set aside some time to develop your perfect investment plan and apply each step with caution if you want to avoid losing your investment.

Lastly, make sure that you are familiar with the services and tools at your disposal so that you can optimize your profits and cut down on the amount of effort and time required to run your investments.

Wholesaling To Retail Workers

You can make a lot of profit in real estate by wholesaling properties, but it is not as easy as you may think. Most experts like to teach wholesaling as a natural means to accumulate wealth without any starting capital. Yes! Wholesaling is a great business, but it often requires some starting capital. This section will help you learn how wholesaling works, what you should expect in the business, and the things that you need to do to be successful.

Many people may not be familiar with the idea of wholesaling real estate, but it is not hard: a wholesaler purchases and sells properties very fast even without doing any rehab, or they receive property under contract and assign the agreement to a different buyer.

Many real estate investors get started in wholesaling because it is an affordable way to generate money. Honestly, many people who want to wholesale, do not earn a lot of money because they give up as a result of the hard work and commitment needed to build an active wholesaling business. The wholesalers who choose to stick to it, and persevere, stand an excellent chance to make millions of dollars from the venture.

So, what is real estate wholesaling

Wholesaling is based on the idea of buying and selling houses in a short period without making any renovations. A wholesaler will look for houses under contract that are below the market value and sell the houses or allocate the deal to a different investor. The wholesaler will sell the house to investors who can then pay using cash because there is no time to receive a loan, and there are no appraisals.

The wholesaler does not need to use their cash because they apply a double close or an assignment of contract. Whenever you double close, the title company will apply the money from the end investor to pay the initial seller so that the wholesaler doesn't assign the contract they had with the seller to the investor, and the investor becomes the buyer.

How does a wholesaler deal take place?

The process involved in a wholesale deal may appear complicated, but it is simple once you determine how the moving parts work and have the right people to assist. Below is how the process happens:

Find the deal

A regular wholesaler may use postcards sent to owners who do not live in the home to attempt to buy the property. Absentee owners are sometimes motivated because they don't stay in the house and may have bad tenants. The wholesaler can also try to search for a deal in many other places, including auctions, FSBOs, MLS, and driving for dollars.

Get the house under contract

Once you find a prospective deal, you need to speak with the owner and get the house under contract. The wholesaler has to be aware of what their investor buyers will cash out for the house and get it under contract for a figure lower than that. The wholesaler creates the difference between what they get the house under contract for and what the buyer is going to pay. To get the property under contract involves the seller and wholesaler signing a contract with all the agreed terms of the agreement.

Look for a buyer to assign the contract to

Once the wholesaler gets the property under contract, they need to look for a buyer. Wholesalers should have names of buyers that they can send the deal to. Every wholesaler is unique in the way they deal with the buyers because some will offer the house based on who comes first, and some may have a bidding system where the best bidder gets the deal.

Set up the closing using a title company

One of the significant features of a successful wholesaling business is to identify an investor-friendly title company. Not every title company will fill a double close or learn how wholesalers work. Most wholesalers demand the end buyer to provide a non-refundable earnest money deposit using their title company. In case the investor pulls out, the wholesaler receives the earnest money.

Determine the closing

The title company has to ensure that the property contains a clear title. Once this is verified, closing is determined, and the title company will generate the paperwork and organize for a day to sign. The wholesaler has to confirm that the house is in the same condition as when the end buyer stated and that the property is accessible and vacant.

There are many steps to follow before a wholesale deal is finalized, and it is not easy (as many people say). The most challenging part is getting deals that are attractive to the end buyer.

What are some of the things that a wholesaler needs to be careful about?

As a wholesaler, your responsibility is to take the title to the house or earn your interest from it. It is not right to introduce a buyer and seller and then only receive a commission. That will be equivalent to brokering the real estate deal, and you must ensure that you are licensed to do this. Keep in mind that it is against the law to be involved in real estate business without a genuine license. That explains why many wholesalers will use a double close to sign a deal or assign a contract. You also need to be careful when sending leads to other real estate agents or investors in exchange for a fee in case the home closes. That is also considered as conducting a real estate business without a license. There could be some instances where you receive payment on a per-lead basis whether the property closes or not. It is essential to get in touch with an attorney for particular legal advice.

How much money can a wholesaler make per deal?

The wholesaler earns money by charging the end buyer more than the amount of money they got the house under contract. The amount of money that they make differs from wholesaler to wholesaler, the type of deal, and many other factors. Some wholesalers only make a few thousand dollars on every deal, while others make $200,000 on a sizeable multi-million-dollar deal. However, some are comfortable with $5,000 per deal, while others close to $20,000 per deal. The wholesalers who earn a lot of money per deal have a longer buyer's list and often get buyers to pay more than the asking price.

How much money do wholesalers make?

Similar to professionals in other industries, some wholesalers know how to work smart and make a large sum of money; others do not work smart and fail. The real estate investors that are happy with the wholesaling venture have different systems in place that help them to find buyers and deals. Some wholesalers make between $20-50,000 per month, but they are not the typical wholesaler. They could be selling between five-ten houses every month to make that vast sum of money. Wholesalers involved in many deals have built a large business. In other words, they are not running this business on their own, but they have a team. For instance, their team will comprise of a contract manager, acquisition person, bookkeeper, marketer, and many more. The wholesalers doing most of these deals also spend a significant percentage of money on marketing. Some send between 10-20,000 pieces of mail every month.

For starters, you can target to sell five-ten wholesale deals in the first year if you dedicate your time and effort. That can translate to a $25-50,000 net income. However, you may not make any money a few months after you start. This should not disappoint you; it is part of the learning curve in any venture that you start. Just remember that it takes time to market-win the heart of sellers, get them under contract, and ensure that the end buyer is willing to purchase the house. You have to remain resilient and optimistic, even when it seems like you aren't going to make it. If you are a go-getter, then you could make a lot of money. Others could make just a few thousand dollars. When everything is not going right, remember that even super successful wholesalers did not achieve success overnight. They had to go through the same troubles you are experiencing. And maybe for them, it was worse. You will need to forego sleep in the first year of your business, so if you are only committing a couple of hours every week, and hope to hit $100,000 per year, then you will be disappointed.

What are some of the common mistakes that wholesalers commit?

Most people who want to become real estate wholesalers rarely do a deal. Some of them have certain misconceptions about how the business operates, and they don't realize the amount of work it takes to become a real estate wholesaler. Below are some of the mistakes committed:

Failing to know what a cash investor will pay

The most critical part of striking a deal is to get a deal. Newbies in the real estate wholesaling business think that because they found a sale by owner or found a seller to call them back, they have won the deal. No! Where you found the property is not essential, but the most important thing is the price you can get the house for. If you do not see cheap properties, none of your buyers will be interested in purchasing them no matter how many names of buyers you have in your contact list.

Crashing for guru promises

Make sure that you don't fall for guru promises. These are promises to get hundreds of wholesale deals or certain access to unlisted foreclosures. Do not be deceived that there is something like special access to unlisted foreclosures. You only get deals from your hard work.

Fudging figures

Most wholesalers try to come up with numbers because they do not know the real numbers or attempt to create something that is not a deal. The best wholesalers work on repeat business, but they don't try to lure investors with bad contracts.

So how can you become a successful wholesaler?

If you want to become successful like a few other wholesalers who are making a ton of money wholesaling properties, then you should be ready to follow some necessary steps to build a robust wholesale business:

- Develop a plan on how you want to market to sellers and buyers.

- Start by creating a buyers list by setting aside time to go and attend REI meetings or look for cash buyers.

- Become an expert at determining values in your location.

- Make an effort to learn how much it can cost to repair properties in your area.

- Begin by marketing properties in your location. Direct marketing can be your best strategy.

- Maintain direct marketing for buyers. The more buyers you receive, the better. The most successful wholesalers never stop searching for buyers.

- Once deals start to stream in, you need to develop systems. Begin by setting different postcards and signs to identify the ones that work best. Look for staff to increase productivity, and create a business that will run without you doing everything.

If the above steps look hard, that is because it is hard. If your goal is to make tons of money in real estate, or anything, you will need to work hard.

How much money can wholesalers pay for houses?

One of the most crucial things about wholesaling a house is to know what your buyer is ready to pay. No one is going to purchase properties if they are highly priced. Most flippers will apply a percent of the ARV to know how much they will pay for a house. The 70% rule is common among flippers. You already learned about this in the previous chapter.

Once a wholesaler is aware of how much an investor can pay for a house, they have to get them to sign a contract. A good wholesaler has to be familiar with values around the place and develop an idea of what it will cost to renovate a house.

How to look for properties to wholesale?

So far, you have learned a lot about why it is essential to strike a sweet deal when wholesaling, but can you do it? Below you will learn the many different ways that you can get cheap properties. Experienced flippers will tell you that they find great deals from auctions, Zillow, Craigslist, and MLS. However, successful wholesalers tend to get their deals through direct marketing:

MLS

Wholesalers can visit the MLS and buy houses, but it is a bit challenging. When you purchase from an MLS, the wholesaler can use a real estate agent, and they may have to involve a double closing. Most MLS sellers, such as the HUD homes and banks, will not permit assignable contracts. A double close happens when the title company uses the end investors cash to buy the house from the original seller. Some sellers will not permit a double close because they have deed restrictions on the timeline in which the property can be sold again after they sell it. It is difficult to commercial foreclosures because of this reason, but some wholesalers have learned how to purchase the LLCs and sell them.

There are different methods to purchase a house from the MLS that is not a foreclosure. Deals by MLS are not accessible to wholesale because many people are aware of them, and most cash investors can purchase the houses without a wholesaler. In case the wholesaler can bargain well or get great deals, wholesaling from MLS could be possible.

<u>Drive for dollars</u>

The drive for dollars takes place when you search for vacant houses while riding your bike, walking, or driving. When you see a vacated house, you get the contact of the property owner and reach out to them to see whether they can sell it for you.

<u>Direct mail</u>

This strategy involves sending letters, postcards, and any other form of correspondence to prospective sellers. You can send out mailers to thousands of homes in your neighborhood. You should use different lists like absentee owners to address people who are likely to sell.

<u>Networking</u>

If you have a network of lenders, agents, contractors, family, friends, and title companies, these can be useful people to help you identify wholesaling properties.

<u>Websites</u>

If you can hire someone to set up an online site for you, you can use this website to attract sellers in your location. That can act as a great source of leads. Still, you have Facebook, Craigslist, and many other social networks to use.

<u>Bandit signs</u>

The simplest way to begin marketing to sellers is to use a few bandit signs, which are signs with the message that you buy houses. Investors prefer to install these signs on busy streets or neighborhoods that they are targeting to buy in.

Auctions

You can also get great deals from auctions, but this can be quite difficult for many wholesalers who use them. Most of the auctions require quick money after the auction is over. It can be challenging to offer an auction contract to finalize a double close. The wholesaler needs to put down a huge amount of earnest money, and they can lose it if they don't close.

For-sale-by-owner (FSBO)

This type of property can act as a great source of deals for wholesalers. You need to do some tasks to find them. Most FSBO sellers have websites to list their properties. You can get FSBOs on Zillow, Craigslist, and Facebook.

Getting deals with little money

Most MLS listings require evidence of funds, earnest money, and a qualification letter. That makes it difficult for wholesalers to purchase from the MLS when they don't have money. Most of the HUD listings and REO do not permit a person to sign a contract. It means that you will need to purchase the property. If you wholesale a property or security because you don't have the cash to purchase a property, it will be difficult to buy a property to wholesale from MLS. If you buy properties from "off-market sellers", then it will be easy to find a house under contract. The seller of an "off-market property" may not need a pre-qualification letter to show before signing a contract.

What does "to assign a contract" mean?

You have heard this phrase used several times when wholesaling properties, but what does it mean? Simply put, the contract contains a clause that authorizes for it to be assigned; in other words, a different person can come in and be the buyer without the permission of the seller. A wholesaler can sell the contract to a different investor without purchasing the house. Anyone can come in and become the buyer as long as they buy it based on the terms of the contract.

How to use a double close to wholesale a house

As a wholesaler, you can purchase a property and sell it straightway without using money. You need to have a great title company that will result in a double close. The seller will sell the house to the wholesaler who shall immediately sell it to the end buyer. The title company will then use the money from the end buyer to pay the initial seller.

How can a wholesaler find buyers?

Most wholesale deals cannot be marketed on the MLS where real estate agents sell properties. You can put a house on sale that you own, and wholesalers don't own the property when they are looking for buyers. They only have the property under contract. That is the reason why wholesalers have to look for both the buyer and deals.

Also, wholesalers must close a deal quickly so that they can assign a contractor to finalize a double close in the contract timeline. They often do not have the time to look for new buyers once they find a deal. However, it is okay if the wholesaler has a buyer's list before they can acquire an agreement. Below are tips to help you find buyers:

<u>REI meetings</u>

 The real estate investor meetups and gatherings are great places to look for investor buyers. You can look for the meetings by searching for local REI in clubs around your place, searching online, or talking to investors.

<u>Look for recent sales</u>

Look in the public databases for anyone who purchased a property recently for cash. These are likely going to be investors.

Hang out where investors purchase properties

Go to places where investors are; these places may include tax sales, auctions, and all great areas where you can find investors.

Advertise

Facebook and postcards on craigslist can be great places. Or even in the newspaper.

Search for other houses to purchase

Many people who are searching for off-market properties are the same investors who buy rentals. Not all of them are wholesalers, so you should look for people hunting deals, and ask them whether they are buyers too.

Networking

Speak to all your local contacts, including lenders, agents, title companies, contractors, etc.

Can wholesalers collaborate with real estate agents?

Wholesalers do not list their houses on the same platform with real estate agents. Wholesalers cannot list the properties not only because they aren't the actual owners, but the wholesaler will have to pay a certain fee to the real estate agent to sell the house. Typically, the wholesaler doesn't have enough room to pay the agent and make money. However, this doesn't show that wholesalers can't work with real estate agents via other means.

Is it possible to become a real estate agent and wholesaler?

Many people believe that you cannot be both a real estate investor and a real estate agent. But it is possible. So, why do people keep saying that investors should not be agents?

Some people believe that it restricts their business to work under the laws and guidelines that real estate agents should work under.

Who pays for the closing costs on a wholesale deal?

When a seller lists a house on sale on the MLS, the seller often pays for some insurance, a few of the closing costs, and the real estate commission. The deals are designed differently when they are wholesaled. The wholesaler will direct the closing cost to the end buyer. If you are the buyer, this is an additional cost that you need to be aware of.

Bird-dogging. What is it?

You will come across the term "bird-dogging" during wholesaling. A bird dog is a person who searches for leads for investors or wholesalers. At one point, we said that it is illegal to receive a commission or fee directly associated with the sale of a house. So bird dogs will often overcome this by accepting a fee for each lead they send to an investor, whether the investor secures the deal or not.

How to get a wholesale deal?

We have talked much about wholesaling a property as an investor. Well, what if you are an investor who wants to purchase wholesale deals? MLS can be a great place to find deals. It takes time to find a good wholesaler. Sometimes, it can be disappointing because there are so many people who say that they are wholesalers but never wholesale a property. So you need to be smart if you want to get wholesalers with the best deals.

How can you purchase a house from a wholesaler?

When a real estate investor purchases a house from a wholesaler, it is different from buying a house from the MLS. The investor does not have a lot of flexibility regarding the extent at which they need to close. Usually, the investor has to commit a non-refundable deposit, and they receive no inspection.

The properties are sold in "as-is condition", and no renovations are done. The following terms can make it difficult to receive a loan on a wholesale deal, particularly when the lender requires an appraisal. It

is difficult to purchase a wholesale deal when you are a new investor because of these constraints.

If the wholesaler has your email, you will receive an email listing the price, terms, and repairs needed. The wholesaler will then compile a list of investors who want to see the home and physically meet the investors at the house.

Every wholesaler does their business differently, so the way they make a decision on which investor gets the property is different. Sometimes, the first investor who asks for the house will get it. Some wholesalers have online forms to use to submit a contract, and the best offer always gets the deal. In case the number of investors is not enough, the wholesaler can decide to negotiate the fee or attempt to get the seller to lower the price.

Don't be overly excited about each wholesaler you come across

The challenge when dealing with wholesalers is that many of them do not do a deal. You will find many people who say they are wholesalers just because wholesaling is the most popular type of investing idea. There are many different types of programs that promise to give you lots of money without using any of yours when you wholesale.

Investors who purchase from wholesalers want a significant discount from what they could buy on the MLS. The wholesaler has to come up with an exciting deal that creates room for them to earn some money and for the investor to also make money. It may take time, effort, and marketing to get these types of deals.

Approximately 90% of the wholesalers don't find a great deal to sell. Below are some of the problems experienced with many wholesalers:

> • They overestimate the market value and underestimate the cost of rehab.

- They can find houses that they think are great deals, but they don't know the market price.

- They don't know the amount of profit that an investor wants on a deal. Most flippers use the 70% rule, and most of the wholesale prices don't offer that kind of benefit.

- They assume that renovations are the only cost on a deal, and forget to include selling costs, etc.

- They don't know how to market or have the money they need to market.

They will avoid disclosing to investors that they have never negotiated a deal—that is why you need to be careful when looking for a wholesaler. You can waste a lot of time with wannabe wholesalers who will never win you a deal. However, when you get the right wholesaler, they can be a great source of the agreement. Do not have high hopes that every wholesaler you come across is going to send you a collection of deals.

How can you find a great wholesaler?

There are different ways to find wholesalers, but not all methods are effective. Here are a few:

Ask around

Some of the best practices to find wholesalers is to network with investors, but they may be severe and not provide you with their source of deals. Apart from investors, you can ask real estate title companies, agents, and others in the business. Many wholesalers like to send an email to real estate agents to look for buyers.

Go online

Many wholesalers own a website for investors who want to purchase deals. You can look online for wholesalers in your locality, but this can be a hit or a miss if they have agreements.

Search for marketers' wholesalers

When a wholesaler is marketing, you will know that they are at least looking for deals. Instead of searching for wholesalers, focus on finding their marketing. Pay attention to bandit signs, Craigslist ads, billboards, Facebook posts, and call the number. Many wholesalers market through advertisements and they will purchase houses fast for cash. Let them know that you do not want to sell your house, but they should include you on their buyer's list. If you get a letter from someone who wants to purchase a house, don't throw it away—call them back and let them know that you are a buyer.

Finding a wholesaler is not easy, but they can serve as a great source of deals. While many wholesalers may not be that good, every market will still have some wholesalers who know how to negotiate for deals.

Wholesaling can be a means to start your investment career in real estate without much experience or money. However, this does not mean that it is a walk in the park, or you will make money fast. It takes much effort, time, and hard work to make millions of dollars from wholesaling properties. Entering the wholesaling business without having enough knowledge can easily make you run into trouble. So you need to take the time and learn how the business operates, learn from successful people, learn your market, look for buyers, and engage in many deals in the right way—and you can be sure to build a successful business.

Chapter 4: Building A Rental Property Empire

Risks Of Investing In Real Estate

Investing in rental properties is one of the best sources of making money and creating wealth. There are a wide variety of benefits that come with owning buying investment properties and generating some passive income from it. However, having a rental property can be a safe investment source, but not every rental investor can achieve success in this industry.

Real estate investing has different types of risks involved, and that is why anyone who is about to invest in rental properties must be aware of them, whether experienced or a newbie investor:

1. The uncertainty of the real estate market

The rental business has been snowballing in the last few years. Despite this, there is no certainty that this trend will proceed. The rental property market is known for its challenges because of the dynamic nature of the market condition. In real estate investment, the market plays a vital role when it comes to financing. For that reason, it is hard to be sure that you will earn a profit when you choose to sell a rental property investment.

For instance, when you buy homes when the demand for houses is high, you could be at risk of selling them at a lower price than the buying price, especially when the demand goes down. That could cost you a lot of cash than what you made while renting the property.

As a result, before you make the final decision to invest in the real estate business, you must first learn about the market. You need to know the current trend of the market and how it operates. Next, you can forecast whether you can make a profit or loss when you sell or buy a rental property. Also, the forecast will help you know the right time for an investment decision.

2. Negative cash flows

In the rental property investment, the cash flow from investment property is any profit size that the property investor will generate once they pay taxes, costs, and mortgage expenses. The next risk that is related to rental property investment is the odds of making a negative cash flow rather than a positive one. In other words, expenses, mortgage payments, and taxes are higher than the real estate income; this may cause one to lose some money.

This risk happens when the investor of property purchases an investment property without doing any analysis of the real estate market. Therefore, the right way to mitigate this risk is by taking the time to calculate your costs and expenses before making any move to purchase an investment property.

It is also essential to ensure that the analysis is in-depth—even small expenses that may seem insignificant add up in the long run.

3. Vacancy risks

Purchasing an investment property does not guarantee that you will have all properties occupied and quick profits. There is a chance that the property will stay unoccupied, which is a significant risk to the investor's rental income because it may result in negative cash flow. Additionally, given that tenants are the source of income in rental investment, a high vacancy is an excellent risk for owners who depend on real estate as the means to pay insurance and other expenses.

To eliminate this risk, rental property owners should buy investment assets in high places that guarantee occupancy. Some of these places can be safe neighborhoods that have amenities.

4. Bad locations

In real estate investment, location is essential. According to rental experts, when buying an investment property, the location should always appear as a top consideration. But how is "place" a danger in real estate?

First, the location will determine the demand and supply. You may think that a particular area is an excellent choice for a rental property due to the affordable prices. However, these places may have many properties with very few occupancies. Hence, investing in these locations may be a big gamble.

Additionally, real estate investors should stay away from areas that have a high incidence of crime. Also, when you invest in a high crime location, the real estate investor is at risk of property damage, which may result in unexpected costs and high costs of repair.

A location will also determine appreciation. When the rate of appreciation is low, then the amount of profit a person can earn when they sell a property is low. For that reason, you should never buy an investment property based on the price alone.

The best way to eliminate this risk is for investors to be careful when selecting a location for rental property investment. Although it could be tempting to buy a cheap home, the risk is not worth it.

5. Bad tenants

Getting tenants is necessary to make money in rental properties investment. But not every tenant will guarantee a profit. This risk might be worse than the risk of having the house remain vacant.

While it is true that having a vacant home may not generate any rental income, a bad tenant can avoid paying rent or even vandalize the property—this means you will need to evict the tenant.

To eliminate this risk, make sure that your tenants go through a rigorous selection criterion before you draw up a contract. Vetting them ensures that you only have quality tenants. A thorough tenant screening process involves looking at their history, credit score, and getting contact information of their previous landlord/s.

6. Lack of liquidity

Liquidity describes the ability to get access to cash that you have in the investment. A risk in real estate investment is that properties are not liquid; in other words, it is not easy to convert the properties into money. Selling a property is not simple and quick, and if you decide to sell quickly, you may likely incur a loss.

The absence of liquidity causes real estate investors to stick to their investments for a more extended period than other forms of investments, which can be a huge gamble for those individuals who want money quickly.

7. Foreclosure

When a real estate investor cannot pay their mortgage on time for a certain period, this may increase the risk of losing the property to the bank. Foreclosures are a significant risk because it affects the ability to get a bank loan approval in the future.

One way you can eliminate the risk of foreclosure is by conducting a real estate market study and property investment before you pay a 20% down payment on the rental property investment.

What Makes A Good Rental Property Investment?

Property investment is the path to long-term profit and growth of capital. However, if you make the wrong choice, it will result in an expensive investment.

Real estate investments are not a means to amass wealth quickly. If you are planning to get into real estate investment, you have to ask yourself many questions, not just "How much will I need to buy a property?".

Simply put, investing in the property only gives you a channel for stability compared to investing in shares and the stock market where you could lose a ton of money in a second. The property offers you a long-term investment and builds a substantial profit.

However, this doesn't occur for everyone. You could end up asking, "Why is property a huge investment?" if your property doesn't generate sufficient profits.

Sometimes, the problem may be the market, but wrong investment decisions are the main reasons.

If you select the wrong real estate property, you cannot expect to make a considerable profit. To stay clear of these problems, look for the following characteristics of a great rental investment property:

Feature 1: The best location

Everybody including experienced real estate investors will mention that location is critical when choosing an investment property. And that is because they are right. It is vital that you ask "How can I find the best suburb for me?" but you will also need to select the best location to get tenants.

It differs depending on the kind of tenants you want. For instance, families will wish for amenities such as schools and leisure facilities to be present, and young professionals want an easy route to reach the city. That means the proximity of your property to the following features plays a key role when it comes to the success of your investment. If you are unable to provide your tenants with what they are looking for, you won't be able to charge a rental fee equivalent to what another investor can.

You also need to consider the growth aspect. Analyze the local economy to learn the condition in which the region is found. A robust infrastructure, or even expected improvements, indicate that a place has the potential to grow and expand. You will also be searching for an excellent educational facility and local business.

Choosing a poor location will restrict what you can charge tenants. Also, if you invest in a rapidly declining region, it will lead to losses when you want to sell the property.

Feature 2: The buying price

Asking yourself, "How much can I spend on a property?" is not sufficient when coming up with the buying price. Keep in mind that you want to make a profit. Just because you can spend more, it doesn't mean you should.

That is the time when a little comparison of the property's buying price to its fundamental value can be helpful. The significant value, in this case, refers to the actual value of the property. Various factors determine it; for example, the yield and growth potential.

The buying price is the amount of cash that you will finally purchase the property for. Everything, including the motivation of the seller and quality of the buyer's agent, can impact this price.

As a rule of thumb, the purchase price must be lower than the intrinsic value of the property. That is the way you generate profit.

Thorough research is the only means that you can use to determine the intrinsic value of the property. Conduct an in-depth analysis and find properties that are on sale for less than this value.

Feature 3: Low maintenance

One of the biggest mistakes that you can make when purchasing an investment property is to buy it without having a rough estimate of how much it will cost to renovate or repair. What are some of the extra costs involved in purchasing the property?

If you are a real estate investor, these costs will include much more than legal and mortgage charges. You need to be responsible for the property maintenance too. If you fail to follow up with maintenance work, you won't attract tenants. Furthermore, you will create a reputation for a poor service, which severely affects the property's potential to generate profit.

Therefore, a substantial real estate investment should have the fewest maintenance problems. Beyond the basics, you do not need to spend much money every month to ensure that it is running.

High maintenance becomes a huge problem when you purchase expensive properties—luxurious properties come with all types of systems and appliances that you will need to keep a close eye on. They require many expenses, which drains your profits.

In this case, low maintenance refers to an investment property that will not eat away your budget with maintenance problems. Keep life simple and pick a security that does not get damaged easily or requires regular maintenance.

Feature 4: Small Flaws

This can look odd to include, but searching for small flaws in the property may be the road to building a great investment property.

This is how it operates. Many investors know that even the least significant flaw will scare away buyers. Most investors want to purchase properties that will generate money right away. They do not want to incur any additional expenses after buying the property.

In other words, you have the least competition when you search for a little flaw. The main thing here is that the flaw must be easy and quick to fix. You don't want to spend too much time trying to repair a property because the investment may increase.

Instead, identify a few small flaws that make the house less appealing, but one which you can fix. Once you fix it, it will instantly increase the value of the property and open channels for new buyers and tenants. Also, you will be spending less than you expected to.

Feature 5: Better rent-to-price ratio

Let's dive into some of the financial features now. Those of you who are planning to invest in making a good profit need to learn how to quote the correct rent. That is what you will be trying to attain. You want to provide tenants with an annual rent of 5% or even less of your property's buying price.

Why is this important?

Many renters compare the advantages and disadvantages of renting versus buying a property. If they are going to spend too much on rent, they may as well decide to give themselves time until they have enough money to buy the property.

However, the correct rent-to-price ratio can limit this from happening.

Let's say that you purchase a house for $400,000. For a 5% ratio, your tenants will pay $20,000 every year. That is a good income, plus it is not that high that tenants can opt to save money for their own homes instead.

A great investment property will allow you to provide a suitable rent-to-price ratio. If yours will surpass 5%, you may end up charging too high. It will exclude you from the market and lower the demand for the property.

Feature 6: Long-term appeal

Market trends will affect the prices of property. A new development emerges, and every investor will want to capitalize on it. Or some building styles become fashionable; this also causes several investors to buy.

Here is the main thing to remember: go for properties that are appealing because of their merits. Essential features such as sizeable bedrooms and storage space don't disappear from the fashion market. Prioritize these feature over the short-term trendy features.

Feature 7: Low vacancy rates

This is related to location rather than the property, but it is still a significant factor to consider.

To make money from your investment, you must have reliable tenants. There should also be some demand for real estate properties.

Therefore, you will always get the best investment properties in places that have low vacancy rates. That shows that the region has a stable local economy, and there is a high demand for properties. Also, low vacancy rates signal that the current landlords do not experience issues with the tenants. If they were, then there would be more evictions, which results in higher vacancy rates.

Also, the low vacancy rate could signal that tenants have the least choices. Therefore, they will be more likely to discover what your property offers.

Feature 8: Fast turnaround from buying to renting

This particular feature is related to the small flaws discussed previously. There is a difference between small flaws and significant flaws. For example, small flaws result in negotiations, and they are easy to repair, but considerable flaws can take months to complete.

The longer you take to fix a problem, the more time you will spend without a tenant occupying your property. When you have an excellent investment property, you will quickly transition from buying to renting it out. And this will begin to return the money you invested, which is the goal of every property investor.

Determine the amount of time it will take to do any repairs. The longer it takes to repair, the less attractive the property becomes.

Feature 9: Not Industry-dependent

Availability of local industry tends to trigger the growth of properties. That occurred in Western Australia during the rise of the mining industry. People relocated to look for work. Sellers and investors made a lot of money since prices soared.

When the boom ended, investors who had purchased properties during the boom period felt the real pain. People started to move away from Western Australia, which reduced the demand for their properties. Owners of properties had no option but to reduce the rents, so that they can retain tenants, and thus allow them to pay mortgages. Repossessions went high when the property of the state burst.

So here is the point: investing in a short-term market economy can result in danger. Keep in mind that property is a long-term investment. For the industry-dependent region, the industry drives the success of the investment. It means that if the industry fails, your investment will be the next thing in line. Therefore, if you have to buy a property in an industry-dependent region, then make sure that several industries are operating in that area.

Feature 10: The nitty-gritty

Your rental property investment must contain little things that tenants search for. Storage space acts as a role than you may expect in tenants' decisions. Simple stuff like a wall space for shelves can make an average investment property become the best.

Modern bathrooms and kitchens also play into the decision-making process. And so too is the size of the bedrooms.

Also, you need to factor in the kerbside appeal. When a property does not look attractive from the outside, the chances are high that it will not grab much attention.

Fortunately, you have the final say on these nitty-gritty things. However, it is crucial that your property gives you the opportunity to take care of it.

As you can see, there's so much that goes into selecting a great investment property. A good location is just the start. You will be searching for multiple industries, which makes sure that tenants have different career options. That will reduce the rate of vacancy, and enhance your rental yields.

The property itself might require some little fixes here and there. These are not a problem as long as you make sure that the turnaround time between buying and renting is quick. If there is a high prospect, and the property does not require much maintenance, you are onto a significant investment.

Remember this advice when searching for investment properties. The best combination of the above features will help you make a lot of income.

How To Buy Your Real Estate Below Market Value

This requires that you be patient and keep working hard to strike a fair deal for a property. Typically, finding a profitable deal is one of the responsibilities of the whole business. But here we shall teach you how to make a significant profit on buying a property. To achieve this requires research, an active transaction, and full commitment.

To be profitable in real estate investment, you must know how to buy real estate properties below the market value and buy properties that will generate high profit. For this, we will start by letting you know the reason why sellers sometimes offer property below market value, the intrinsic value, and finally, how you can buy land below the market value.

So, why do sellers offer real estate property below the market value?

Nobody ever wants to offer their property below its value. If an individual does, then there must be a specific reason. In most cases, the reason revolves around time. Sometimes, choices can be emotional and irrational. For instance:

- Personal problems.
- Facing budgetary problems.
- Facing a foreclosure with a financial institution.
- Interested in a different property.

- To share funds with a legatee.

- Re-locating because of work-related problems.

When you come across a dealer who is dangerous on a short-term sale, this is a golden chance for you to accept the deal with the cost and terms of the contract on your side.

In the following case, never feel shy to ask, "What is the reason for the sale?" and "For how long has the property been listed?" Getting to know these nitty-gritty aspects will create a clear idea of how much room you have to enter into a negotiation because your deal will turn out to be pretty simple.

What Is The Intrinsic Value?

The intrinsic value or the market value is the original price that the property would be sold for based on its present condition. The side of the business determines this cost, or it could depend on the personal interaction between the seller and the buyer. Keep in mind that it is not agreed like the price of a product in a retail shop. There is just one method of determining the estimation of a property if you are not an agent, and that is by comparing similar deals. You have to look for recent offers of comparable properties around the area. One of the most accurate methods is to do it yourself. Similarly, the least demanding style to find the market value is to look for service supplies. They will require a complete liability to give you a lucrative deal.

Keep in mind that if you are searching for a property that requires repairs, then you have to get it at a much lower cost—unless you are not buying at lower market value.

Strategies For Buying Real Estate At A Low Market Value

To purchase a real estate property, be aware that there are short sales below the market price, fair market deals, off-market properties sold below market value, and auctioned property. When your primary goal is to take advantage of buying real estate lower than the market value, make sure that you go to these properties.

Short sales are a popular hotspot for financial experts. Private vendors own short sales, but the vendor must pat the bank more than the amount they are asking for the home. With a particular goal in mind to sell a house, the bank has to agree to accept less money than they are owed. Short sales last for six months or a year before being closed. And one of the reasons is that sellers do not jump to a conclusion. They take their time to agree on a particular choice.

Fair market deals refer to properties claimed by a private vendor who has a say in the property selling decisions. They can offer it without involving the bank. It is challenging to identify fair market deals because the merchant is not in a hurry to provide their home below the market value. There are a few instances where you can come across a great deal for a fair market sale.

Most service providers aim at a property that has not been listed for sale because they believe that it may not cost them the actual market price, and they could easily earn some profit. These are like off-market properties because they are not available for purchase. You need money and investment to have the ability to purchase these types of properties.

When a seller dispossesses a house, it is a must for one to make an effort and reclaim its miseries before assuming the responsibility of the property. This kind of property is called auctioned property. It is one of the reasons why many homes are unloaded at the steps of the courthouses so that you can quickly know when your local courthouse runs the auctions and grab the most lucrative deal from it as soon as possible.

That said, do not let go deals in which the vendor uses the following terms:

- Divorce

- Desperate merchant

- Distressed property

- Decreased estate

- Induced seller

In general, to determine how to buy real estate below market value, you will need to be ready to do a lot of work and dedicate some time in in-depth research. So after adopting the following techniques, your deal can be highly profitable.

How To Repair And Maintain Rental Properties

We have talked much about how you can invest in real estate, or how you can purchase a rental property, yet what most people do not talk about is the need to take care of their rental properties. When you are healthy, you need to keep fit to ensure that you remain healthy, and it is the same with your rental property investment. It requires special attention and intensive care for you to be successful and stay successful.

So how can landlords and rental property owners repair and maintain their properties? What should they do to keep up with regular occupancy in their real estate?

Owning a rental investment property can be highly profitable and a great source of passive income. It generates a lot of cash flow to investors to the extent that after paying all the bills, they are still left with a significant profit. Those who run or own a rental property investment have the opportunity to dictate their success or failure. They have the power to control the situation and their financial future. One way of increasing your success and cash flow from your rental investment is learning how to repair and maintain it. There are several advantages to doing this. A property that is well maintained retains its intrinsic value and grabs the attention of tenants hunting for homes, which benefits both parties.

Here are some tips to help you repair and maintain your rental investment property:

1. Check the interior and exterior sections of your real estate

By ensuring your rental property is well kept and free from any form of vandalism will increase your income and let you retain good tenants. Unexpected costs, such as repairs and replacements, are unavoidable when managing real estate, and you should not ignore them. Below is a compilation of things that you need to identify in a rental property:

Exterior

> • Roof: Find out whether there's any mold, moss, missing shingles, and a damaged flashing. All of these may lead to expensive repairs. You should also inspect to identify whether any tree limbs stretch onto your roof and remove them. You want to ensure that you don't have any of these because they can chase away potential tenants.

> • Windows: Inspect your windows to ensure that they are sealed correctly with no gaps; if you find such gaps, seal them. It will save you from future damage by the moisture and heat released.

> • Paint the exterior: verify that the outer section of your rental property is painted to protect it from any sun damage and moisture. Nobody wants to move into a house that looks dull or bad on the outside.

> • Landscape: inspect for trees that have fungus, or broken tree branches. Anything that may cause harm to your tenants should be fixed. Also, make some effort to cut the grass and let it look healthy.

Interior

> • Smoke detectors: This is a must. Always inspect your smoke detectors to verify that they have new batteries and are working correctly. It can be very risky to live in a house with smoke detectors that aren't working correctly.

- Water heater: Make sure that you drain and regularly remove any dirt inside the water heater. If you stay in a region with a lot of solid particles in the water, you can consider making this a monthly routine task.

- Heating and cooling: You should ensure that you check the heating and cooling system often. Inspect the filters and ensure that no plants are growing around them. That can prevent air flow and destroy the system in the future.

- Paint: Look for any paint chippings that may be on the walls and make sure to repaint the walls for a fresh and neat interior.

2. Hire a property manager

If you find managing your rental repairs and maintenance tasks overwhelming, then you can hire a property manager. Real estate investment demands much of your time; if you feel like it is too much, then a property manager could be the best person to handle the tasks on your behalf. This one is a big decision to make because you will need to pay the property manager, but think about all the time it is going to save you. A property manager can do everything that you want from interior to exterior, including handling the monthly rent.

3. Make your tenants happy

Another way that you can maintain your rental property investment is by making sure your tenants are satisfied and happy. Just a simple checkup to know how they are doing, or asking whether they need any help, will do the trick. Showing them that you are concerned, and their happiness is your priority, will make them happy. That will build your reputation as a good landlord and attract potential tenants to your property. Make sure that you are quick enough to act on their repair requests. One of the primary reasons why tenants move out and search for a different home is because they are not happy, so make sure that your tenants are satisfied.

4. Respect the landlord-tenant law

Respecting the landlord-tenant law ensures that you manage and maintain your rental property investment. This law will act as a structure for both you and your tenants so that no one makes mistakes, and it keeps your real estate in excellent condition. One of the requirements of this law is maintenance.

5. Renovate and enhance the property

Everyday tenants look for new and developed rental properties. As the landlord or property owner, you should always look for ways to renovate and improve the appearance of your rental property. For instance, adding a new type of design to the exterior side, adding a garden, or even modernizing the interior section by installing frameless walls. These new changes will grab the attention of tenants, including those who are not searching for a house.

In short, tenants need to enjoy a safe and conducive environment, and the property owner must repair and maintain the property. A well-maintained property will increase your cash flow and success. Always look for methods to solve rental property problems before they become big.

How To Build A Rental Property Empire

If you want to scale your rental investment portfolio like an expert and build your rental property empire, you will have to seek an investment partner. If you are going to do it yourself, then consider this: if you can generate money by yourself and an investment partner's money, will that not be a significant achievement?

Your investment partner will add some value to your investment that you currently don't have. If you want to learn how you can scale your real estate investment, here is a solid blueprint:

Step 1: Begin by investing in real estate

Let us burst some bubbles with this first step. You need to at least be successful in real estate investment to manage to find a partner to invest with. If you have not yet invested in yourself, then it will be wholly irresponsible to use someone else's money.

Real estate investors will be attracted by two significant things: your level of expertise and your success stories. That means lacking any deals under your belt could show that you do not have the experience, or you may not know what you are doing. Besides, it shows that you haven't been disciplined enough to create and save enough of your cash to invest in a deal. Neither is going to look well for a real estate investor.

Step 2: Develop a first-class real estate team

It is crucial to assess the people you do business with most of the time. Whether it is a realtor, contractor, or plumber, anyone that you are working with should add value to your process, unlike doing a transaction.

Your team has two functions:

1. They should ensure that a real estate transaction is as smooth and predictable as possible.

You need to work with the best people from your region, and not your friends who work in the business. At this point, the focus should be to receive wins on your record. If you have an unfortunate result from a personal investment, then that is a less successful story for you to sell to a rental property investor.

2. They work as extensions of your business that you can point others to.

Step 3: Position yourself as a resource

You need to establish yourself as a rental property investor that people trust and depend on for help with anything in the real estate.

As you continue to assist people in their real estate transactions, your reputation will begin to grow in the community. And the word will start to spread.

Keep in mind that your first goal should be to attract a money partner that is going to help you. The main word here is a resource. You are not trying to show that you are an expert by taking a big game. Get interested in other's real estate transactions, be authentic and helpful, and they will speak good of you.

Assisting others will make you an expert quickly

By being of help to your friends and network, it will add to your experience. You will acquire intimate knowledge of the neighborhoods they enter, and naturally, they'll improve on some of the processes you gave them.

Step 4: Turn each conversation into real estate

People must know that you are a real estate investor. However, this does not mean that you post every success story on Facebook or Instagram; no one likes that. What you need to do is to make sure that people in your network know you as a savvy investor. When people become interested in your real estate investments, it is a good practice to let them invest.

Encourage people to realize it's possible

Sometimes, a simple thing like just saying, "We could buy something together" can start a conversation that may lead somewhere great. The more you continue to grow on your own, the more questions people will keep asking you. And this will result in more opportunities.

The things that you should remember is that you need to invest in real estate actively, and you must succeed in doing it.

Investors want to work with professionals. If you hold a position where people are displaying interest in working with you, it could be because your efforts have shown results.

Don't damage it by avoiding the little details

Presentation is important. Fortunately, it is not hard to look professional. Now is the best time to begin building a brand. You may think like you are faking it but disregard those thoughts. The truth is that this is another self-evaluation in your journey of what you have decided to achieve.

Step 5: Build your digital presence

First, create a website: You can do it on your own or hire a web developer.

Business cards: This is also something that you can do on your own. Make sure that you have these cards ready when you attend any social or business meetings.

Build your highlight package: Here, you should outline all your digital transactions.

Step 6: Behave and act like a real estate professional

Now that you look like a real estate professional, it is time to act like one. Ensure that all email communications go through a business email.

Qualify your leads

Most of the focus until now has been on presenting yourself to a partner. However, you don't want just any partner—because you are going to work with the following person financially in the years to come. Protect yourself by checking to confirm that your leads are okay before you introduce them to your whole sales process. You will achieve this by asking questions throughout the entire communication.

Some important things that you need to determine include:

- Do they have enough capital to channel it to real estate?

- What types of real estate investments do they have experience with?

- How fast do they expect ROI?

- Is there anyone who would be involved in the decision-making process?

- What level of participation are they willing to provide?

Asses the skill set you bring to the table, identify what you need from a partner, and walk away in case the prospective partner doesn't qualify.

Step 7: Closing the deal

If you have found that the partner is fit to work with you, it is time to begin building a relationship while continuing to demonstrate your skill sets.

Learn to be educative

You can begin by sending the real estate partner listings you see as interesting. Send them short summaries of the cons, pros, and cash flow projection of the properties. Teach them insights of inspecting a transaction—that will generate confidence in the partner.

If the partner begins to send you listings and asks for your opinion, that is great. It is a sign that someone has invested and is happy.

As you can see, there is a lot that you need to do to build a real estate empire. There is no easy or straightforward blueprint. So make sure that you do not waste your time and money going to attend seminars that promise you this will happen overnight. Concentrate on optimizing your growth first and becoming the version of you that will attract partners.

Work hard to become a professional now, then build your brand so that you look successful when leads start to arise. Know the value that you generate, and determine the kind of partner you want to expand your business with. Spend time on evaluating your leads and save everyone time in the long term.

Chapter 5: Tips for Finding Quick Profit Deals

How To Find Real Estate That Will Offer You Passive Income

Many people will ask whether it is possible to invest in rental properties passively. Let us find out how you can invest in rental properties passively and how you can choose the best passive income investments.

We know that to make money, one must work unless they win a lottery ticket. However, that does not come easily. One thing with working is that if you down your tools, you stop getting money, or if you quit your job, the money you used to receive stops flowing. That aside, there are different ways that you generate an income without doing much of the work. Most people refer to it as "generating passive income." So, passive income can be described as the money you make by pumping your money in a project while other people work on it. Each member gets their share when the income trickles in.

So, when we talk about "passive income" regarding real estate, we are pointing to investing your cash in a rental property and letting others handle the work for you. So you can sit back, and wait for the money to flow.

However, the most disturbing question is: "What are the methods through which you can identify the best passive income investments when it comes to real estate?"

There are several rental property investment methods that you can use to generate passive income. In this section, we shall share a few strategies to find the best passive income rental investment:

1. Look online

If you search online for the best passive income investments, you will come across many online platforms that have specialized in this sector. That said, here are a few real estate platforms that you should consider as passive income investment opportunities:

● Fundrise.com: This one is among the best rental investment platforms online that accept real estate investors from different parts of the United States. The best thing about Fundrise is the way they have a diversified commercial real estate portfolio. This particular feature makes it possible for rental property investors to accept to invest their cash in a low-risk project. It does not matter how much money you have; all you need to do is invest and then present the share of capital that you can manage.

● RealtyShares: This is another dominant real estate online platform. It gives you the ability to identify the best passive income investment. One thing that sets apart RealtyShares is that you can get into the real estate investing business and decide whatever investment property type you want to invest. They have a wide variety of investment properties from single-family homes to massive apartment buildings.

2. Get the best passive income investments through real estate firms

When we talk about real estate firms, we refer to turnkey real estate investing. In other words, you invest in a rental property that has already been repaired, so it is ready for a person to move in. As a result, you get the chance to buy the property as it is with the tenants. In most cases, the rental property comes with professional property management services.

So why is a turnkey real estate property a passive income stream?

Purchasing a property that already has professional property management to handle repairs and maintenance is a passive income investment. But that does not imply that you don't invest any energy or time into it. Keep in mind that this is one of the real estate investment methods that require minimum effort. As a result, you will have a rental property that provides you with rental income at the end of every month while the property manager is running the daily operations.

3. By investing in rental properties

Another method that you can choose to make money passively in real estate is through rental properties. You have the option to invest in long-term or short-term rentals. No matter the real estate method you select, a rental property is one of the best ways to earn passively in real estate. This type of property originates from low risk and a steady rental income.

If you are still trying to understand what makes it a passive investment, this is the point where professional property managers come in. So, for it to be a passive investment, you will have to hire a professional property manager. This manager should be experienced in matters to do with rental properties. They will ensure that the property expenses go down while optimizing the rental income. Therefore, they will help increase the profit of your rental business.

4. Real estate partnerships

Real estate partnerships have shown to be the ways for one to earn passively in real estate. If you do have the money to invest, but you do not want to participate in the physical work, then you should consider financing with a partner. Look for someone ready to invest the effort while you offer the funds. After all, you are presenting the partner with the financial resources they didn't have.

5. Real estate crowdfunding

Real estate crowdfunding is very popular among real estate investors who want to generate money passively. Real estate crowdfunding is a means of raising funds for real estate investment projects, whether it is a real estate development project or a rental property investment. You can participate in it regardless of the size of the money you want to invest.

Also, real estate crowdfunding lets you access real estate syndicates. Crowdfunding has been one of the means through which real estate syndicators receive financial resources. That way, you can invest the amount of money you want and earn a passive income in exchange. The one thing that makes it the best passive income investment is that you do not need to commit your effort at all. The syndicator handles everything, including all the responsibilities involved in the venture. In other words, you are only funding the real estate syndicate.

How To Find Quick Profit Deals

Rental property investors are informed consumers. Every time a great deal presents itself, investors are pushed to pass it. After all, a real estate bargain is the best opportunity to optimize profits.

So the cheaper you get a property, the higher the ROI is. But getting such a deal is not as easy as it seems. New investors, for example, may experience a hard time when negotiating for a real estate deal. On the other hand, experienced investors can identify a profitable deal when they see one as long as they know where to search for it.

Foreclosure Deals

This is one of the most popular ways of acquiring cheap and profitable sales. For those who have mastered how to navigate around the process, this could be a grand bargain.

For those that are still not familiar with the idea of foreclosures, there is one thing that you need to remember: a foreclosure happens when the owner of a property fails to make payment for their property. Failing to pay your property will be considered as loan default. Although the foreclosure process highly depends on the condition of the property, most of the states will release a default notice in case the owner fails beyond 90 days. After this, the loan is sent to the foreclosure section.

The appearance of foreclosure is lucrative to a rental investor. The price tag connected with each often represents a significant discount—because time is essential for the owner. However, when you know that you can pay for a house at a lower value than its current price, that should tell you that you aren't the only one wanting the property.

Since foreclosures are released to the public, getting one is not easy because of the competition. To eliminate any "busy work", real estate investors are encouraged to focus on properties that are in the "pre-foreclosure" stage.

Investors must win the approval of the seller—this is not easy. The real estate business involves networking.

Before negotiating, investors are advised to follow all the due diligence when looking for deals. Do not move forward before doing the correct research on the home in question. It is during this time that you need to learn everything about the property. Most importantly, make sure that there is no obstacle or challenges that will act as a barrier during the process of the transaction. Once the cost is okay, get in touch with the homeowner and organize for an appointment. Keep in mind that the owner already has a Notice of Default. That means you will have to negotiate the terms, join escrow, and close the deal before the property is set for a public auction.

If done correctly, purchasing pre-foreclosures can be the most profitable ways for an investor. On the flip side, it is one of the most misunderstood.

Auction Properties

When looking for profitable deals, auction sites could be another great place to secure a deal. Although it is not that popular as a foreclosure, it is easy to understand. One thing that you should know is that auction property has an attractive budget. There are two ways that a property can be listed for auction: one, the owner of the property stops paying taxes for the house; or two, the property enters into foreclosure. In general, homes that have been listed for auction usually have a starting bid that is less than or equal to the balance left on the mortgage. The process will take place fast. Hence buyers must be quick enough to act.

Just like any auction, home auctions have some risks involved. But the risk is balanced by the final reward that one gets. Investors who want to purchase an auctioned property from homeowners are advised to do comprehensive research. That way, they will know how much to spend on the property.

Do not forget that auctioned properties require payment by cash. However, there are some exceptions. Every municipality and auction firm has its methods. That said, be aware of what to expect early.

Bank-owned REOs

As long as a home does not sell at auction, the chances are that the bank will own the property. This is referred to as an REO (real estate owned) property. These assets taken over by the bank are a huge bargain for homebuyers. Of importance, however, is the degree of safety by which the above properties are sold.

For that reason, these types of properties can be one of the safest deals in the whole market. Because the bank owns these properties, the bank will handle the repairs, and taxes that were a problem.

Finding And Funding Your Property

Many people have the ambition and knowledge to become investors, but there is only one thing that they lack: the capital. Accumulating all the cash together before you can start in real estate can be very tough, especially if you are young. However, once you overcome this barrier, you can be sure to be in business.

It does not have to be that difficult. If you can translate your creativity and resourcefulness into some serious thinking, you can come up with creative ways to finance your rental investment properties. Below are a few things that you can do to get that capital:

Inspect your pocket first

No one can have a few thousand dollars and fail to know. If you want to invest in rental properties, you must be serious about personal finance, and you are likely to feel like you have done a lot to save something.

However, there are always means to cut down your expenses without affecting your lifestyle. For instance, you can revisit your phone service provider and find out whether you can get free data or even lower the price. Also, join reputable real estate websites and learn how you can save money. In other words, look for ways to live the same way you are living now by just spending low.

Once you can free up some money, you will develop a better idea of how much you can dedicate to your property. You could be in for a big surprise.

Get to know about other people's financial capacity

Another option is to take on investment partners.

All cash

It is the king of all financing tactics. Cash is king, and in real estate that is true. If there are two offers presented to a seller, and one option is conventional financing, while the other one is all-cash, the seller will prefer the all-cash deal. The reason is that cash is quick, and there are no financial institutions that could come in and stop the agreement. This option is one of the best to sellers because it is the easiest type of financing method. While this could be a great way to buy your properties, it is not the best method to get an ROI.

Conventional mortgage

To include a mortgage on real estate means that you apply for a loan from a financial institution, such as a bank, that pays the buying price minus the deposit you placed on the property. That means if you purchase a home for $100,000, and pay a down payment of $10,000, the loan that you need to pay is $90,000—and you will have to make payments each month until you clear it.

The bank accepts to do this because they earn interest on the money they lend you. The majority of conventional mortgages ask for a minimum 20% down payment, and some may require between 25%-30%.

Conventional mortgages always have the least interest rate of all kinds of financing options. There is a different time interval to select: ten, 15, 20, and 30 years. The longer the period, the more interest you are going to pay.

FHA Loans

This is a loan from the Federal Housing Administration, one of the departments of the US Government that is responsible for ensuring mortgages for banks. The banks receive insurance on the money that they give you to buy a property. This loan is strictly meant for owner-occupied properties and not for investment properties.

The importance of the following loans is the minimum down payment of about 3.5% of the buying price. Taking into consideration that a conventional mortgage minimum rate is 20%, you will be able to pay for a lower down payment to move to get the property. It is good because you will get a higher ROI because you committed less money on the property.

While the FHA loans are designed for owner-occupied alone, there are ways to get around this and use it in the investment strategies. For example, if you purchase a property to stay in using an FHA loan, after one-two years, you can refinance the loan to get out of the FHA loan. Next, you can purchase the second property using a new FHA loan and then the rent out the first home. You can still use this FHA loan to buy a duplex, or even a four-plex if you decide to live in one of the units and rent out the rest.

However, the FHA has some negatives too. You can only have a total of four FHA loans. This means that once you own four homes plus paying a mortgage, you won't manage to buy another home using an FHA loan. Another disadvantage is that each month you pay the mortgage, there is a charge called Private Mortgage Insurance. It is the money you pay the bank's insurance for the money they lent you.

You will be paying for insurance the same way you do for car insurance, but this one goes to the FHA department for insurance just in case you avoid paying the loan.

Owner financing

In this financing model, the owner of the property becomes the bank. The agreement would be to let the property owner hold the note against the property the same way a bank does if they lent you money. In this case, you will negotiate with the property owner the interest rate and terms. Since the lender is the owner, they will probably have their conditions for you, such as a balloon payment, interest rates, down payment, and other forms of requirements.

It is not worthy as an investor to apply owner financing if the seller owns the property "free and clear" or the mortgage of the property is an assignable loan. The "free and clear" is one where the owner does not have any remaining mortgages linked to the house and owns the property outright. The "assignable loan" is where the owner can hand over his or her rights and obligations to you as the buyer.

You are not advised to buy a property using owner financing in case the mortgage cannot be assigned. Owner financing can be a great way to own property using little or no money because the owner is in control. You don't need to be worried about the lenders, or any possible hang-ups that can stop you from getting the property.

Hard money

This is a type of loan that originates from the private business or individual that you can get to invest in rental property investment. Hard money has several advantages over other kinds of finances, but it does have some limitations. Some of the benefits include no credit references, no verification of income, and the deal can be financed in a few days.

The disadvantages include a short-term note of three-six months, and a higher interest rate of more than 15%—more loan fees to find the loan.

How To Grow Your Portfolio To Have Multiple Investments?

When any reasonable person thinks about investing in real estate, they will start to think about getting their first investment property. Thinking about the first real estate is the driving force that makes any real estate investor start in the crowded industry of real estate.

Buying your first investment property could be the first step that any real estate investor makes to expanding his or her rental investment portfolio.

Investors should remember that generating money in a rental investment is a gradual process, just like building your real estate investment portfolio. The most successful real estate investors started their journey with little or even no money, but the most important thing is not how much you begin with but what you do with what you have.

Planning

Before starting any venture, rental property investors should be ready to make decisions that they believe will bolster their financial prosperity. On the flipside, getting started in real estate without any preparation or plan may lead to one making wrong decisions, which can result in financial losses.

The most successful rental property investors have a vision that assists them in developing the real objectives that can be implemented into a plan. The plan, when executed in the right way, can breathe life into the real estate investor's vision. To expand your real estate investment portfolio, you need to develop a vision of what you believe would be the right real estate investment portfolio and make decisions that will move you closer to your vision.

The main thing with planning a real estate investment portfolio is the math for your real estate investment. If you would like to know how you can become rich in rental property investment, it is as easy as learning and mastering math. Math in rental property investment is critical because you need to compute the financial features of the investment.

Determine Your Finances

Evaluating your financial status and coming up with creative strategies to finance can boost your rental investment career. As mentioned previously, to become rich in real estate requires that you master all the math of investing, which can be considered the financial characteristic of investing. Developing a business plan to stick to can be achieved in many ways. One method that a beginner real estate investor will depend on is getting finances through relatives and people in trusted networks.

Getting a down payment for the first rental property is the secret that opens the gate to success in real estate investment portfolio. To get a clear picture of how this can be a powerful trick, buy your first property, get tenants, then begin to look for another. That is the way it should follow in most cases if you want to expand your rental property investment. Getting that first investment property is the channel to building multiple rental properties.

Diversify Your Real Estate Portfolio

It is crucial for investors to diversify their selection. When you expand your investment, it reduces the risks and increases returns. Building a diversified rental property investment portfolio demands investors to scan through multiple investment techniques to be familiar with the factors that can set apart properties. For that reason, a real estate investor must know how to diversify their portfolio geographically.

When you have a geographically-diversified investment, it could imply that you have many things in different forms. It could also mean having investment properties in different regions.

A popular investment strategy is to diversify the types of real estate one chooses to invest in. In other words, you do not restrict yourself to one specific type of investment property but own different types of investment properties that will deliver regular income under any condition. A real estate investment portfolio is said to be diverse when the investor owns and controls different types of rentals like single-family homes, office rentals, and multi-family homes.

Consider Learning A friend

One thing that sets apart successful rental investors is their ability to remain resilient and healthy even after failing. They move forward and learn the correct way to deal with challenges. The best advice for any rental property investor, especially the ones that are about to build a real estate portfolio, is to continue learning. Keep reading books, browse websites, and attend conferences and meetings. Learning is an essential tool because the market keeps changing. Learning any factor that affects real estate can be handy in the long term. In-depth knowledge on matters to do with real estate investment can provide the investor with the required expertise to identify off-market properties and translate leads to actual expenditures.

The real estate investment market is a packed market. It requires investors to build a sustainable real estate investment portfolio that is diverse enough to get the benefits of it. Using these steps to expand your investment portfolic will require patience and commitment.

Conclusion

Thank you for making it through to the end of *Real Estate Investing: An Essential Guide to Flipping Houses, Wholesaling Properties and Building a Rental Property Empire, Including Tips for Finding Quick Profit Deals and Passive Income Assets*. It should have been informative and provided you with all of the tools you need to achieve your goals, whatever they may be.

Real estate has a great track record. Investing in rental properties provides the opportunity to earn a huge return and create meaningful diversification to your investment portfolio. When handled wisely, it can be a valuable tool of cash flow in your investment portfolio. Just like any other investment, real estate is not an exception; you need to understand and measure the risks and expected rewards before starting.

Depending on how you decide to invest in real estate, you will require a different amount of capital, time, knowledge, and patience.

If it matches with your goals and personality, high-risk house flipping ventures may be what seems right for you. If you do not have in-depth knowledge, capital, or experience to start house-flipping, you can choose to go with property wholesaling, which doesn't require much capital. If not, you can still access the diversification benefits. There are several passive investment options in real estate investment that can assist you to unlock real estate without many obligations.

Finally, if you found this book useful in any way, a review on Amazon is always appreciated!